# RANGERS
## 100 HEROES

## THE AUTHOR

**Dean Hayes** took up full-time writing after a career in teaching and a spell as a professional cricketer. He has written over 80 sporting books, including *Scotland! Scotland! The Complete Who's Who of Scotland Players since 1945*, *Northern Ireland's Greats* and *Living the Dream: Manchester City*.

# RANGERS
## 100 HEROES
### of the MODERN GAME

**Dean Hayes**

**MERCAT PRESS**

First published in 2007 by Mercat Press
Birlinn Ltd, 10 Newington Road, Edinburgh EH9 1QS
*www.mercatpress.com*

Text © Dean P. Hayes, 2007

ISBN-13: 978-1-84183-125-1
ISBN-10: 1-84183-125-5

Set in Ehrhardt with headings in Gill Sans at Mercat Press

Printed and bound in Great Britain by Antony Rowe Ltd

# CONTENTS

# ILLUSTRATIONS

# INTRODUCTION

It arose in conversation while researching this book. Just how many players have pulled on a Glasgow Rangers shirt since the Second World War? It was a question that, while not impossible to answer, would tax even the most dedicated of Rangers historians. A thousand? Twice as many? Not as many as a thousand? All that can be said with any certainty is that a lot of footballers have had a unique privilege bestowed on them. The very act of running on to the park as a Rangers first-team player ought, by definition, to confer hero status. They tread where the rest of us can only dream.

Being asked to write a brief summary of the club's modern-day heroes is easier said than done. After all, football is completely subjective and we all have our own ideas as to who would comprise the top 100 and who would not.

Also, on what criteria do you decide who to include? Is it the most skilful? The most popular with the fans? The most loyal? The parameters are endless. In the end, it came down to a number of factors. It was not necessarily the most talented, not always the most obvious individuals, but players who have all made a major contribution to the post-war history of Glasgow Rangers Football Club in one way or another.

In the years immediately after World War Two, Rangers' famous 'Iron Curtain' defence helped the Ibrox club maintain their dominance of the Scottish game. The Jim Baxter-inspired side of the 60s swept everything before them, although it wasn't until the following decade that they were able to overturn Celtic's nine-year supremacy and capture two 'trebles'. There followed a number of lean years, but then, reinvigorated by Graeme Souness and a number of English imports, and afterwards by Walter Smith in 1997, Rangers famously matched Celtic's 'nine in a row'. Under Dick Advocaat, the Light Blues captured five out of six Scottish trophies between 1998 and 2000. Following the reigns of Alex McLeish and Paul Le Guen, Walter Smith is now back in charge at Ibrox, renewing Rangers' challenge to Gordon Strachan's Celtic.

While exceptional footballers such as Willie Thornton, Willie Waddell, George Young, Jim Baxter, John Greig, Ally McCoist and Brian Laudrup have all played leading roles in the club's history, the Light Blues have always prided themselves on their great teamwork.

This book is not for the football anorak, more just a passing glimpse into the career highlights of 100 men who have graced the Light Blue shirt of Glasgow Rangers. Apologies to all those players and former stars who have been omitted, and if you don't believe me when I say it was an extremely difficult task to whittle the selection down to 100 names, try it yourself!

Dean P Hayes

# JORG ALBERTZ

**Born:** Monchengladbach, Germany, 29 January 1971
**Rangers career:** 1996 to 2001
**Appearances and goals:**

| League | | FA Cup | | Lg Cup | | Europe | |
|---|---|---|---|---|---|---|---|
| **A** | **G** | **A** | **G** | **A** | **G** | **A** | **G** |
| 141/15 | 58 | 17/2 | 5 | 12 | 7 | 31/11 | 12 |

*Total appearances:* 201/28
*Total goals:* 82
**League Championships:** 1996-97; 1998-99; 1999-2000
**Scottish Cup:** 1998-99; 1999-2000
**League Cup:** 1996-97; 1998-99
**Honours:** 3 German caps

The Hammer will always be a hero with the Rangers fans for his brilliant close control and the explosive power in his left boot. Few had heard of the hugely talented German when Walter Smith paid Hamburg £4 million for his services, and Albertz found himself in the awkward position of having to fill in at left-back for much of his first season at Ibrox.

He started out with Fortuna Dusseldorf, but when the team from the Rhineland were relegated to the Second Division of the Bundesliga, Albertz moved to Hamburg SV. Here he soon became a popular figure and was made club captain two seasons after his arrival at the club. It was here that he acquired his nickname of 'The Hammer', primarily for his powerful long-range shooting.

In 1996, Jorg Albertz signed for Rangers, helping the club to a ninth Championship title in a row and scoring a famous free-kick against rivals Celtic. Those goals set the Light Blues on their way to a stunning 3-1 victory in the '97 traditional Ne'erday derby fixture, and went a long way in securing the historic nine-in-a-row Championship achievement by Walter Smith's side. In the last league game of Smith's final season in charge, Albertz was sent off, which meant he suffered the heartache of missing the Scottish Cup Final.

Albertz became a huge favourite with the Rangers fans, but following the departure of Walter Smith in the summer of 1998, he was frequently left out of the starting line-up by the incoming Dick Advocaat. During the club's Championship-winning season of 1998-99, Albertz netted a spectacular hat-trick for the club in a 6-1 home win over Dundee.

He also produced some superb European displays, scoring vital away goals at PSV Eindhoven and Beitar Jerusalem for example. For a big man, Albertz had great feet, and though he wasn't the quickest of players, he could ghost past opponents as if they were not there. He was a regular destroyer of Celtic!

In 2001, Albertz was sold back to Hamburg for £3.5 million, later citing Advocaat as the main reason for his departure from Ibrox. Despite the hype of his return, he was unable to live up to the expectations, and just before the start of the 2002-03 season, he moved to Shanghai Shensua, a team from China. Having had only moderate success in China, he moved back to Germany in 2004 with Greuther Furth. On the receiving end of a number of injuries, he then returned to his first club, Fortuna Dusseldorf.

## LORENZO AMORUSO

**Born:** Bari, Italy, 28 June 1971
**Rangers career:** 1997 to 2003
**Appearances and goals:**

| League | | FA Cup | | Lg Cup | | Europe | |
|---|---|---|---|---|---|---|---|
| **A** | **G** | **A** | **G** | **A** | **G** | **A** | **G** |
| 148 | 13 | 20/1 | 5 | 13 | 2 | 40 | 4 |

*Total appearances:* 221/1
*Total goals:* 24
**League Championships:** 1998-99; 1999-2000; 2002-03
**Scottish Cup:** 1998-99; 2001-02
**League Cup:** 1998-99; 2001-02; 2002-03

Lorenzo Amoruso was a target for most of the premier clubs around Europe during the 1996–97 season, and so it is to the credit of chairman David Murray and manager Walter Smith that Rangers emerged at the head of the bunch.

Having had three spells with his home-town club Bari, with brief interludes at Mantova and Pescavo, Amoruso moved to Serie A giants Fiorentina in 1995. He was a linchpin of their side, which went all the way to the semi-final of the European Cup-Winners' Cup. A powerful stopper, he gave Ronaldo one of his toughest matches of the season when the Italians played Barcelona. Rangers cannily played on the fact that Fiorentina needed to repay a large chunk of the transfer fee invested in bringing Andrei Kanchelskis from Everton, and moved in with a bid which the Florentine club could not refuse.

The real drama, came, however, when Manchester United topped Rangers' offer on the day that Amoruso was due to sign, but the Italian flat refused the opportunity even to speak to United and chose to complete his deal with Rangers, which he felt, thanks to the work of Murray, was much more attractive to him.

He made his league debut against Celtic, but played in only four league games in that 1997-98 season, as an Achilles injury, picked up while still playing in Italy, plagued his early days at Ibrox. He did make a brief appearance in the Scottish Cup Final in May 1998, but Rangers lost 2-1 to Hearts and ended the season without a trophy. Early the following season he was appointed captain by manager Dick Advocaat, and picked up his first trophy when St Johnstone were beaten 2-1 in November 1998. The Light Blues went on to complete a domestic treble with Amoruso as skipper by winning the Scottish Premier League title and then the Scottish Cup by beating Old Firm rivals Celtic.

The Scottish champions were knocked out of the UEFA Cup by Borussia Dortmund, and Amoruso was caught on TV appearing to mouth racial abuse at Nigerian Victor Ikpeba. Amoruso admitted a racist taunt and apologised for his actions.

In 1999-2000, Amoruso skippered Rangers to a second Premier League title, but missed the Scottish Cup Final win over Aberdeen through injury. Despite losing his place on the arrival of Dutch Euro 2000 star Bert Konterman, Amoruso turned down a move to Sunderland and vowed to fight for his place. Later stripped of the captaincy following a dismal 3-0 home defeat by Kilmarnock, he continued to be an important member of the team and was a member of the Rangers side that won the League Cup in March 2003, beating Celtic 2-1. Later that season, he won a third Championship medal with Rangers in the closest title race in history, after a 6-1 victory at home to Dunfermline, and ended a memorable campaign by scoring the only goal in Rangers' Scottish Cup victory over Dundee.

In the close season, Amoruso completed a £1.4 million three-year deal with Blackburn Rovers, but his progress at Ewood Park was hampered by a heel injury that required surgery. At the end of the 2005-06 season in which Amoruso failed to make an appearance, he was released.

## SHOTA ARVELADZE

**Born:** Tbilisi, Georgia, 22 February 1973
**Rangers career:** 2001 to 2005
**Appearances and goals:**

| League | | FA Cup | | Lg Cup | | Europe | |
|---|---|---|---|---|---|---|---|
| A | G | A | G | A | G | A | G |
| 74/21 | 44 | 11/3 | 6 | 5/3 | 4 | 13/2 | 3 |

Total appearances: 103/29

Total goals: 57

**League Championships:** 2002-03; 2004-05
**Scottish Cup:** 2001-02; 2002-03
**League Cup:** 2002-03
**Honours:** 53 Georgian caps

Georgian international Shota Arveladze started his career in his homeland with clubs like Iberia Tbilisi and Dinamo Tbilisi, before joining Turkish side Trabzonspor. A solid and reliable striker, he finished as top goalscorer at least once at each of those clubs. When he topped Trabzonspor's goalscoring charts in 1995-96, he also led the Turkish Premier Sup League, making him the second non-Turk to date to lead that league in goals after Tarik Hosie in 1983-84.

On leaving Trabzonspor, Arveladze signed for Ajax and spent five seasons with the Dutch giants. His impressive form on the continent brought him to the attention of a number of top clubs, but it was Rangers who won the race for his signature, paying £2 million for his services in September 2001. Arveladze, whose involvement in the Champions League meant he appeared in both legs of the qualifying tie against Celtic, scoring in Amsterdam, was then forced to sit out Rangers' UEFA Cup campaign.

He made his Rangers debut in October 2001, scoring twice, the first a stunning 5th minute opener in the 3-0 defeat of Airdrie in the third round of the League Cup. In his next match—a home league game against Kilmarnock—Arveladze emphasised his talent by scoring the first goal and making the other two in a 3-1 victory. He ended his first campaign with an impressive 17 goals in 29 games in all competitions.

He continued to be an important goalscorer, and the following season netted a hat-trick in a 4-3 home win over Livingston. That 2002-03 season saw him play a crucial role in the Rangers team that pipped Celtic in the race for the SPL title and win medals in both the Scottish FA and League Cup Finals. Arveladze, who scored the 3000th goal in the SPL, announced, after not being offered a new deal, that he would be leaving Ibrox when his contract ran out in the summer of 2005. Even, so, he promised to leave on a high by trying to help Rangers win another title. He had missed out on the CIS Insurance Cup Final through injury, but did score in the quarter-final defeat of Celtic. In the run-in to the League, he scored twice in the penultimate game of the season as Motherwell were beaten 4-1, and went on to pick up his second Championship medal.

A regular in the Georgian national team and his nation's all-time leading scorer, he returned to Holland in the close season, signing for AZ Alkmaar. Following an outstanding season, having netted a hat-trick in a 5-0 defeat of RBC Roosendaal in February 2007 and helped his side to the knockout stages of the UEFA Cup, Arveladze parted company with the Dutch club, signing for Spanish league Levante UD.

## SAMMY BAIRD

**Born:** Denny, 13 May 1930
**Rangers career:** 1955 to 1961
**Appearances and goals:**

| League | | FA Cup | | Lg Cup | | Europe | |
|---|---|---|---|---|---|---|---|
| A | G | A | G | A | G | A | G |
| 121 | 39 | 16 | 2 | 26 | 6 | 16 | 5 |

*Total appearances:* 179

*Total goals:* 52
**League Championships:** 1955-56; 1956-57
**Scottish Cup:** 1959-60
**Honours:** 7 Scotland caps

A graduate of the famous junior football academy Rutherglen Glencairn, Sammy Baird was a powerful left-sided player who began his career with Clyde. He became a senior professional with the Bully Wee, helping them win the 'B' Division Championship in 1951-52 as they finished a point ahead of runners-up Falkirk. One of Clyde's most consistent performers, he had represented the Scottish League XI and come close to winning full international honours when, in June 1954, Scot Symon, manager of then First Division Preston North End, paid £12,000 to take him to Deepdale.

After making his debut in a 3-1 home win over Arsenal, he kept his place for the game against Sheffield United, but failed to get on the scoresheet in a 5-0 win for North End. Though he scored against Sunderland and in the derby game with Blackpool, he found it hard to settle in the English top flight, and when Symon returned to Rangers as manager, he bought Baird for a second time, at the slightly reduced price of £10,000.

Baird made his Rangers' debut on the opening day of the 1955-56 season, in a goalless home draw against Stirling Albion. He ended the campaign with 14 goals in 33 games, including a hat-trick in a 4-0 home defeat of Airdrie, as the Light Blues went on to win the League Championship. Baird continued to use his physique—5ft 11in and 12st 8lb—to good effect over the ensuing seasons, often being quite an intimidating player. He helped Rangers retain their title in 1956-57, and although his goals' tally was down, he helped create numerous chances for the likes of Max Murray and Billy Simpson.

It was certainly an unwise decision to foul Sammy Baird. Known as the 'Straight-backed SB' due to his upright running style, this and his shock of blond hair made it quite difficult to ignore him on the field.

His form for Rangers led to him winning the first of seven full caps for Scotland, when he scored on his debut in a 2-0 win over Yugoslavia. A member of the 1958 Scotland World Cup party, he was, prior to the 1990 World Cup competition, the only Rangers player to have scored in the World Cup finals.

Very much a type of inside-forward long identified with the Ibrox club, he scored in the Scottish Cup quarter-final win over Hibernian in 1959-60 as Rangers went on to win the trophy, beating Kilmarnock in the final. Though classed as more of a provider, he had still managed to find the net 52 times in his 179 games for the Ibrox club before leaving to have spells with Hibernian and Third Lanark, prior to being appointed player-manager of Stirling Albion. He led them to promotion to Division One in 1964-65, but was sacked after relegation three seasons later.

# MICHAEL BALL

**Born:** Liverpool, 2 October 1979
**Rangers career:** 2001 to 2005
**Appearances and goals:**

| League | | FA Cup | | Lg Cup | | Europe | |
|---|---|---|---|---|---|---|---|
| A | G | A | G | A | G | A | G |
| 47/6 | 1 | 2 | 0 | 5 | 0 | 10/2 | 1 |

*Total appearances:* 64/8
*Total goals:* 2
**League Championships:** 2004-05
**League Cup:** 2004-05
**Honours:** 1 England cap

---

Probably my most controversial selection, Michael Ball's Rangers' career was sadly hampered by a troublesome knee injury.

Having graduated through the ranks at Everton, Ball made his Football League debut in a crucial relegation battle against Spurs. Showing maturity and composure in his play well beyond his 17 years, Everton caretaker boss Dave Watson had no qualms about introducing him after just 23 minutes into a fierce Merseyside derby. A sharp-tackling, overlapping left-back and possessing a long throw, Ball proved equally at home in central defence, and it was these qualities that later allowed Howard Kendall to sell Andy Hinchcliffe to Sheffield Wednesday.

In his first full season in the Premiership, Ball was called up to the England squad for the friendly against Hungary and represented the Under-21 side. He then suffered a loss of form and had trouble in convincing manager Walter Smith he was worth a starting place in a full-strength Everton side. His development as a player though was acknowledged by Sven Goran Eriksson, with a first full cap against Spain in February 2001.

Allowed to leave Everton, primarily because of the Merseyside club's financial problems, Ball had offers from other Premiership clubs, but opted for a lucrative deal with Rangers. He moved to Ibrox in a £6.5 million deal, making his debut alongside fellow newcomer Shota Arveladze in a 3-0 League Cup win over Airdrie. Four days later he played in his first SPL game as Kilmarnock were beaten 3-1. A few games later, he had a very public and well-documented spat with manager Dick Advocaat after he was substituted during his first Old Firm match against Celtic. His early days with the club were further marred by medial ligament damage which kept him side-lined for 18 months.

Ball had taken injections in the final months of his Everton career and pulled out of several England Under-21 squads, but following exhaustive tests and a visit to a Belgian specialist, Rangers were told his knee was in 'excellent condition' and signed him on a five-year contract.

Upon his return to fitness, he scored his first SPL goal, having netted in an earlier UEFA Cup match, in a 2-0 win at Dundee. Having regained his place in the side, he won a SPL Championship medal in 2004-05 and helped the Light Blues win the League Cup by defeating Motherwell 5-1. The last in a long line of problems with his time at Rangers was when the club refused to play him, as Ball was about to hit the number of matches played that would trigger the final instalment of his transfer fee to Everton. It is to the player's credit that he agreed a deal with Everton whereby he would personally make a payment towards the outstanding sum every time he set foot on the park for Rangers.

In the summer of 2005, Ball moved to Dutch side PSV Eindhoven, as the Ibrox club were keen to remove the higher earners from their wage bill. Despite winning a League winners' medal in his first season, he was, at the start of the 2006-07 season, deemed to be surplus to requirements by new PSV boss Ronald Koeman. Having impressed on a week-long trial with Manchester City, Ball signed for Stuart Pearce's side and scored his first goal for them in the FA Cup tie against Preston North End. Having stamped on Ronaldo in the Manchester derby, Ball, who apologised for his attack, has now been offered a new two-year contract.

## JIM BAXTER

**Born:** Hill o' Beath, 29 September 1939
**Died:** 14 April 2001
**Rangers career:** 1960 to 1965 and 1969 to 1970
**Appearances and goals:**

| League | | FA Cup | | Lg Cup | | Europe | |
|---|---|---|---|---|---|---|---|
| **A** | **G** | **A** | **G** | **A** | **G** | **A** | **G** |
| 150 | 19 | 21 | 0 | 54 | 2 | 29 | 3 |

*Total appearances:* 254
*Total goals:* 24
**League Championships:** 1960-61; 1962-63; 1963-64
**Scottish Cup:** 1961-62; 1962-63; 1963-64
**League Cup:** 1960-61; 1961-62; 1963-64; 1964-65
**Honours:** 34 Scotland caps

There is little argument that Jim Baxter was the most incredibly gifted footballer ever to pull on the light blue shirt of Rangers. He was a quite exceptional footballer of world class, and he proved it time and time again with astonishing ball skills, particularly with his left foot. For five years he was the king of the all-conquering Rangers side put together by Scot Symon, and he relished the adulation. The bigger the stage, the better it suited 'Slim Jim'.

Born in the Fife village of Hill o' Beath, the young Baxter served a brief apprenticeship as a cabinet maker in the nearby town of Dunfermline before succumbing to the fate of most working men in such a small coal-mining community—he went down the pit. It wasn't long before he became a part-time player with Raith Rovers, keeping his job on at the pit. He was one of the last of the young men of that era to do National Service, which he did in the Black Watch.

It soon became evident that Raith would be unable to hold on to such precocious talent, and in the summer of 1960 and with a number of clubs expressing interest, Rangers boss Scot Symon gave Rovers a cheque for £17,500 and Baxter was on his way to Ibrox.

Jim Baxter was certainly a player for the big occasion. He loved the Old Firm matches, and loved 'taking the mickey' out of Celtic when he could. Perhaps the most vivid example of this was the replay of the 1963 Scottish Cup Final, when Rangers demoralised Celtic with a 3-0 win. Indeed, Baxter had a remarkable record in these matches. In the period 1960–1965, he played 18 times for Rangers against Celtic, ten league matches, five in the League Cup and three in the Scottish Cup, and was only twice on the losing side!

He also had his own style. There was a rule in those days that Rangers players must have their shirts tucked inside their shorts. Baxter, however, always left a small part hanging outside over his left hip. It was a distinctive trademark and went with the swagger about his movements that marks only a few players as being of the highest class. Baxter would often skip training if he had been out on the town the night before, and such scenarios would exasperate manager Scot Symon. But Symon knew that if he dropped him, the Rangers fans would soon be on his back.

Capped 34 times by Scotland, he was a member of the 1963 Scottish side which overcame the handicap of losing Eric Caldow with a broken leg to beat England 2-1. Baxter scored both the Scottish goals that day. In October of that year, to celebrate the centenary of the Football Association, England played a Rest of the World side at Wembley. There was a glittering array of talent from across the globe, with Eusebio, Puskas and Yashin all taking part, but displaying as much skill as any of the famous names was Jim Baxter. In 1967 Baxter inspired Scotland to a 3-2 victory over the reigning world champions—black and white television footage of Baxter teasing the England defence with an astonishing display of ball control is still shown to this day.

In the last season of his first spell at Ibrox, Baxter broke his leg during a 2-1 European Cup tie victory over Rapid in Vienna in December 1964. He was out of action for over three months, and by the time he had regained full fitness, he had become restless. Feeling that he was worth more money than Rangers were prepared to offer him, he was particularly angered when a deal with Spurs fell through. Eventually, in the summer of 1965, Baxter signed for Sunderland for a fee of £72,500.

The Wearsiders were hardly setting the First Division alight, and after a less than happy time at Roker Park, Baxter joined Nottingham Forest for

*Jim Baxter in action for Rangers (www.snspix.com)*

£100,000. He was by now no longer being selected for the international side, and it was no surprise that his spell at the City Ground lasted less than two years. Given a free transfer, the great man, who was becoming more known for his off-field activities, unexpectedly received an offer to return to Ibrox and play once again in the light blue shirts of Rangers.

The move back was a big mistake, for the years of drinking and gambling had taken their toll—sadly, Baxter was a pale imitation of the player who set Scottish football alight less than decade before.

Tragically, Jim Baxter lost his fight with cancer at the age of 61, and football lost one of its greatest sons. Glasgow Cathedral was packed for a moving and most entertaining funeral service. His coffin was carried into the great edifice by six of his former team-mates, and the Ibrox club's players and management past and present were among the mourners.

## JIM BETT

**Born:** Hamilton, 25 November 1959
**Rangers career:** 1980 to 1983
**Appearances and goals:**

| League | | FA Cup | | Lg Cup | | Europe | |
|--------|--------|--------|--------|--------|--------|--------|--------|
| **A** | **G** | **A** | **G** | **A** | **G** | **A** | **G** |
| 104 | 21 | 18 | 2 | 24 | 6 | 6 | 1 |

*Total appearances:* 152
*Total goals:* 30
**Scottish Cup:** 1980-81
**League Cup:** 1981-82
**Honours:** 25 Scotland caps

Jim Bett's route to Ibrox was one of the strangest ever trodden! The Hamilton-born midfielder was an associate schoolboy with Dundee prior to signing for Airdrie. It wasn't too long before he was transferred again, this time to, of all places, Valur FC of Reykjavik, Iceland, for £1,500. It was while playing for Valur that Bett met and married an Icelandic girl, but moved on and up to SK Lokeren of Belgium.

The move to Lokeren proved to be the catalyst for a significant upturn in the midfielder's fortunes, as John Greig paid £180,000 to bring him to Ibrox in the summer of 1980. On his arrival at the famous ground, Bett made an immediate impact on the Rangers team with the quality and control of his play. He was, however, never wholly accepted by the fans, who recognised him as highly capable but not as consistent as he might be. Even so, his form for the Light Blues earned him the first of his 25 full caps for Scotland when he played in the 2-1 defeat of Holland.

Bett was a two-footed, intelligent, skilful player with a killing first touch on the ball. In a sense, he might have been a little before his time at Ibrox, when the Rangers team played a more vigorous game than the more tactical approach which came a little later in the decade. Like the England international Ray Wilkins, Bett was not inclined to release the ball until he was sure of its target. In that respect, Jim Bett preferred the simple pass, and this was his main quality over his three seasons with the club. Bett won a Scottish Cup winners' medal in his first season with Rangers, as Dundee United were beaten 4-1 in a replay, and then, in 1981-82, picked up a League Cup winners' medal as the same opposition were defeated 2-1. In the semi-final second leg against St Mirren, after the first game had ended all-square at 2-2, Bett opened the scoring from the penalty-spot in a 2-1 win for the Gers.

In 1983, domestic reasons took him back to Lokeren, where he spent a further two years before Aberdeen persuaded him back to Scotland at a cost of £300,000. The early months of his Pittodrie career were hampered by a variety of injuries, but once he regained full fitness, his artistry and vision in the middle of the park quickly established him as a great favourite with the Dons fans. He marked his first season at Aberdeen by the lifting of the Scottish Cup, playing a prominent role in the 3-0 final success over Hearts. He remained a first team regular and, in 1990-91, when Aberdeen pushed Rangers right to the infamous last day at Ibrox for the League title, he was the only Aberdeen player to feature in all league matches.

He continued to play for the Dons for a further three seasons before injury and the arrival of much younger team-mates limited his appearances and he left Pittodrie to continue his career with Hearts. Virtually an ever-present in 1994-95, he then spent a year at Tannadice helping Dundee United out of the First Division, before retiring from playing.

## RONALD DE BOER

**Born:** Hoorn, Holland, 15 May 1970
**Rangers career:** 2000 to 2004
**Appearances and goals:**

| League | | FA Cup | | Lg Cup | | Europe | |
|---|---|---|---|---|---|---|---|
| **A** | **G** | **A** | **G** | **A** | **G** | **A** | **G** |
| 81/10 | 30 | 9/3 | 2 | 8 | 1 | 18 | 5 |

*Total appearances:* 116/13
*Total goals:* 38
**League Championships:** 2002-03
**Scottish Cup:** 2002-03
**League Cup:** 2002-03
**Honours:** 67 Holland caps

When Ronald de Boer joined Rangers for £5 million in August 2000, the attacking midfielder was an experienced Dutch international who had played under the then Rangers boss Dick Advocaat in the 1994 World Cup Finals, and had won a European Cup winners' medal with Ajax when they defeated AC Milan in 1995. De Boer's arrival was a great coup for the Ibrox club, and demonstrated that the Light Blues could not only attract some of the world's finest players, but were also extremely serious about competing at the highest level in European football.

After starting his senior career with Ajax, de Boer had two years with FC Twente before rejoining the Dutch giants. Following their success in the

Champions League, De Boer, who was a regular in the Dutch side, scoring 13 goals in 67 appearances, left to join Barcelona in a high-profile move. He had played in six games and scored twice for Holland in the 1998 World Cup Finals, though he did miss a penalty in the penalty shoot-out against Brazil in the semi-finals!

His time at Barcelona saw the usually prolific goalscoring midfielder find the net just once in 33 outings, and rather than spend his time warming the bench, he opted to join the Dutch legion at Ibrox under the manager, his countryman, Dick Advocaat. Among the Dutch internationals who then played for Rangers when he joined were Arthur Numan, Bert Konterman, Fernando Ricksen and Giovanni van Bronckhorst.

De Boer burst onto the Ibrox scene with a powerhouse of a display against Sturm Graz in the Champions League, but was reduced to hobbling out of contention for the serious part of the season against lowly Brechin City on Scottish Cup duty. However, when he did return he netted in the last two games of the season against Kilmarnock and Hibernian. Though his hunger was questioned in 2001-02 as he toiled to build on his first few displays for Rangers, he later proved himself to be an integral part of the club under Alex McLeish. De Boer was a key man in the Rangers side that won the Scottish Premier League, Scottish Cup and Scottish League Cup in 2002-03, helping the side claim a place in the group stages of the Champions League at the start of the following season. One of his best performances in that historic campaign came in the game at Tannadice against Dundee United, where he scored two goals and had a hand in two others in the 4-1 win.

De Boer scored a number of vital goals, including three in Old Firm fixtures. In October 2002 he netted with a flying header from a Neil McCann cross at Parkhead, then two months later scored the second in Rangers' 3-2 win at Ibrox. The following April his goal in the 2-1 defeat to Celtic meant a two-goal swing in terms of goal difference that in the final analysis proved critical.

Having spent four successful seasons with the club, he decided to join Al-Rayyan after he was informed his contract would not be renewed after the 2003-04 season. He has since moved on to Al-Shamal, being reunited with his brother Frank, his team-mate at Ajax, Barcelona and Rangers.

## KRIS BOYD

**Born:** Irvine, 18 August 1983
**Rangers career:** 2006–
**Appearances and goals:**

| League | | FA Cup | | Lg Cup | | Europe | |
|---|---|---|---|---|---|---|---|
| A | G | A | G | A | G | A | G |
| 44/10 | 39 | 3 | 5 | 2 | 1 | 8/3 | 3 |

*Total appearances:* 57/13
*Total goals:* 48
**Honours:** 9 Scotland caps

Rangers completed the signing of the SPL's leading scorer Kris Boyd from Kilmarnock in January 2006. The 22-year-old put pen to paper on a three-and-a-half year contract at Ibrox after Kilmarnock agreed a compensation package worth in the region of £500,000 with the Scottish champions. Boyd, who was also a target for Cardiff City and Sheffield Wednesday, revealed that the chance to play in the knockout stages of the Champions League persuaded him to snub a move south to England.

Boyd started his career with Kilmarnock and made his debut for the Rugby Park club on the last day of the 2000-01 season against Celtic. The following season, following the departures of Ally McCoist and Christophe Cocard, Boyd was given more of a chance to stake a place in the team. In 2002-03 he scored 12 times and won the club's 'Young Player of the Year' award. He was also a regular in the Scotland Under-21 team, and in 2003-04, netted 15 times.

The goals continued to flow, and the following campaign he almost set a record for himself when he scored all five of Kilmarnock's goals in a 5-2 defeat of Dundee United. This equalled the record number of goals scored in a single match set by Kenny Miller, who scored five against St Mirren for Rangers in 2001. In fact, Boyd did have the ball in the net six times, but the referee blew up for an infringement.

He was in blistering form at the start of the 2005-06 season, and in December it was announced that he would sign for Rangers in the January transfer window. In an unusual move, he waived half of his £40,000 signing-on fee, which Kilmarnock were due to pay him under the terms of his contract, to help fund the youth set-up which benefited his early career.

He made his Rangers debut against Peterhead in the Scottish Cup third round, netting a hat-trick in a 5-0 win. Another treble followed in a 4-1 win at Dundee United, as he went on to score 20 goals in 17 starts in the second-half of the season, to total 37 between the Gers and Kilmarnock. Boyd was also the first player to finish top scorer at two clubs in one season, having scored 17 goals for Kilmarnock before his move.

His form that season led to him winning full international honours for Scotland, when he scored twice in a 5-1 win over Bulgaria in the Kirin Cup. Boyd extended his fine international form into European Championship qualifying, scoring two goals in Scotland's opening match against the Faroe Islands.

Having been suspended for the first match of the 2006-07 season, he was left out of the starting line-up by new manager Paul Le Guen. On his return to the side, he netted both Rangers' goals in a 2-0 defeat of Hearts, but

*Kris Boyd completes a hat-trick against Aberdeen in 2007 (www.snspix.com)*

after scoring a penalty against Motherwell, he was involved in controversy. Following a dispute between Le Guen and Barry Ferguson, resulting in Ferguson being stripped of the captaincy, and dropped from the team, he held up six fingers after scoring in a defiant show of solidarity for Ferguson, who wore the No.6 jersey. After Le Guen and Rangers parted company, Boyd scored a double in Walter Smith's first game back at Ibrox against Dundee United. In February 2007, he netted a hat-trick against his former club in a 3-1 win for the Gers, and continued scoring throughout the season, including another treble against Aberdeen. He scored his 100th SPL goal and his first against Celtic in the 2-0 Old Firm victory in May 2007.

## RALPH BRAND

**Born:** Edinburgh, 8 December 1936
**Rangers career:** 1954 to 1965
**Appearances and goals:**

| League | | FA Cup | | Lg Cup | | Europe | |
|---|---|---|---|---|---|---|---|
| A | G | A | G | A | G | A | G |
| 206 | 127 | 33 | 29 | 54 | 38 | 24 | 12 |

*Total appearances:* 317
*Total goals:* 206
**League Championships:** 1958-59; 1960-61; 1962-63; 1963-64

**Scottish Cup:** 1961-62; 1962-63; 1963-64
**League Cup:** 1960-61; 1961-62; 1963-64; 1964-65
**Honours:** 8 Scotland caps

Ralph Brand lies third in the Ibrox post-war strikers' list behind Ally McCoist and Derek Johnstone, with a total of 206 goals in 317 games. He is also the only man to have scored in three successive Scottish Cup Finals, four if you include the fact that one of those Finals went to a replay!

As a 15-year-old, he played for Scotland against England in a schoolboy international at Wembley. These were the early days of television, but the match was broadcast and among the viewers was Bill Struth, the legendary Rangers manager. Struth already knew about the young Brand from his scouts, and in that summer of 1952, signed him on a provisional contract. Brand turned professional in the spring of 1954 and made his debut at the age of 17 at outside-right. The match was against Kilmarnock—Rangers won 6-0 and Ralph Brand scored twice.

He spent most of the next couple of seasons doing his National Service, but by December 1957 he was back in the Rangers side. He quickly established a striking partnership, known as M and B, with centre-forward Jimmy Millar, and ended the 1957-58 season with 14 goals in 28 games. The following season he netted 21 goals in 25 league outings, including netting his first hat-trick in a 6-3 win at Queen of the South. Injuries hampered his progress in 1959-60, but in one of the few games he did play, he scored four in a 6-1 League Cup win at Hibernian.

His best was yet to come, and in 1960-61, he was ever-present in all League and Cup matches, scoring a total of 40 goals in all competitions. The total included a hat-trick in the league game against Third Lanark which Rangers won 4-3, the League Cup semi-final when Queen of the South were trounced 7-0, and, in the quarter-final of the European Cup Winners' Cup, as Borussia Moenchengladbach were defeated 8-0 at Ibrox! As well as his four goals against Hibernian, he netted four in a 6-0 League victory over Raith in 1961 and against East Stirling in a League Cup tie in 1963. Such was his form in 1962-63 that he also scored hat-tricks in consecutive games against Kilmarnock and Raith.

But it was in the Scottish Cup that he left a record goalscoring mark. In the 1962 Final he netted the opener in a 2-0 win over St Mirren, whilst the following year he scored the Rangers goal in a 1-1 draw with Celtic, prior to netting twice in the 3-0 replay win. Then, in the 1964 Final, he wrote himself into the record books by getting another goal as Dundee were beaten 3-1.

Ralph Brand put so much into a match that he'd often be found sitting in the dressing-room a full hour after the final whistle, still anxious to talk about it! Brand was a deep thinker on the game, wanting to talk tactics and eager to do extra skills training. He scored six goals in eight international appearances, and was perhaps unlucky to be a contemporary of the great Denis Law.

His last appearance for Rangers was on the final day of the 1964-65 season, when he scored the only goal of the game against Third Lanark. With the Rangers team beginning to break up, he was allowed to join Manchester City in the close season for a fee of £30,000. He ended his first season at Maine Road with a Second Division Championship medal, but after a season in the top flight, he moved to Sunderland.

While at Roker Park, he qualified as an FA coach, later returning to Scotland to see out his career with Raith Rovers. He then had a brief spell as manager of Darlington, the Quakers experiencing one of their worst-ever campaigns under his charge in 1972-73! Brand resigned after they had just defeated Yeovil Town in the re-election poll, to take over the reins at Albion Rovers. He later coached Dunfermline Athletic before working as a taxi-driver.

## GIOVANNI VAN BRONCKHORST

**Born:** Rotterdam, Holland, 5 February 1975
**Rangers career:** 1998 to 2001
**Appearances and goals:**

| League | | FA Cup | | Lg Cup | | Europe | |
|---|---|---|---|---|---|---|---|
| A | G | A | G | A | G | A | G |
| 72/1 | 13 | 9/1 | 3 | 6 | 1 | 26 | 5 |

*Total appearances:* 113/2
*Total goals:* 22
**League Championships:** 1998-99; 1999-2000
**Scottish Cup:** 1998-99; 1999-2000
**League Cup:** 1998-99
**Honours:** 67 Holland caps

The ability to adapt is crucial for footballers who understand the value of versatility to a manager—and to their career. Giovanni van Bronckhorst is one such player. Given he can be classed as left-back, left-wing back, a left midfielder or a left-sided central midfielder, it is hard to know what the Dutchman's best position is.

Having started out with RKC Waalwijk, he had made his mark with Feyenoord when Rangers paid the Dutch club £5 million for his services in the summer of 1998. He was already a regular international when he joined the Light Blues ,teaming up with compatriot Dick Advocaat, the Ibrox club's new manager. In his first competitive game for Rangers, a remarkable UEFA Cup tie away to Irish League side Shelbourne, van Bronckhorst marked his debut with a finely struck goal as Rangers came back from 3-0 down to win the match 5-3. Later that season, he netted the opener in the second round first leg 2-1 win over Bayer Leverkusen.

Used mainly as a play-making midfielder, van Bronckhorst helped Rangers to two successive League Championships, his skill and subtlety making him an important member of the side. Unfortunately the popular Dutchman was ruled out for three months in 2000-01, having picked up a groin injury in a World Cup match against Cyprus. His influential presence was sorely missed as the Gers crashed out of the UEFA Cup in the third round to Kaiserslautern, and failed to reach the final of both domestic cup competitions.

In the summer of 2001, van Bronckhorst opted for an £8.5 million move to Premiership Arsenal. Arsene Wenger had signed the Dutchman to replace the midfield void left by the departure of Emmanuel Petit, and he was expected to partner Patrick Vieira in the centre. However, his period at Highbury was marked by a cruciate knee ligament injury which saw him sidelined after only a few months at the club. When he returned, his role was increasingly minimal and he found himself more on the bench than the pitch. He didn't leave the Gunners without any silverware, however, as he collected a Premiership and FA Cup winners' medal.

As the 2003-04 season approached, van Bronckhorst had the opportunity to move to Barcelona and work with new boss Frank Rijkaard as part-exchange for the transfer of Cesc Fabregas to Arsenal. After adapting to his new role as left-back, he helped Barca to a revival in the second half of the campaign. He won the La Liga title with Barcelona in 2004-05 after some of his finest displays, and repeated the feat the following season, while winning the Champions League as well.

Having made his national debut in August 1996, he has since gone on to earn 67 caps, including two World Cup and two Euro Championship campaigns. In the game against Portugal in the 2006 World Cup Finals, he received his marching orders in a match that saw four red cards given—a World Cup record. Interestingly, van Bronckhorst was seen watching the closing minutes while sitting next to his Barca team-mate Deco of Portugal, who was issued a red card moments earlier! A clause in his contract said that he could return to Feyenoord, the club he supported as a youngster, and he rejoined them in the summer of 2007.

## BOBBY BROWN

**Born:** Dunipace, 19 March 1923
**Rangers career:** 1946 to 1956
**Appearances and goals:**

| League | | FA Cup | | Lg Cup | |
|---|---|---|---|---|---|
| A | G | A | G | A | G |
| 211 | 0 | 33 | 0 | 52 | 0 |

*Total appearances:* 296
*Total goals:* 0
**League Championships:** 1946-47; 1948-49; 1949-50
**Scottish Cup:** 1947-48; 1948-49; 1949-50
**League Cup:** 1946-47; 1948-49
**Honours:** 3 Scotland caps

Bobby Brown was the first great Rangers goalkeeper of the modern era, keeping 109 clean sheets in the 296 games he played. He also had what was then the most unusual habit of making sure he turned out with a new pair of white laces in his boots for every one of his matches!

Tall, blond and agile, Bobby Brown was the last line in a famous Rangers defence which became known as the 'Iron Curtain', and also featured Sammy Cox, Ian McColl, Jock Shaw, Willie Woodburn and George Young.

He had started out with Queen's Park, playing his first match for them against Celtic at Parkhead in April 1940. A crowd of 50,000 witnessed a memorable game which ended all-square at 4-4. During the Second World War, Brown served in the Fleet Air Arm and 'guested' for a number of Football League clubs, including Chelsea, Chester, Plymouth Argyle and Portsmouth. Towards the end of the hostilities, he won international honours when selected to play against England at Villa Park. Facing the likes of Lawton, Matthews and Mortensen, Brown produced a number of top-class saves, though the Scots went down 3-2.

With the war over, he enrolled at Jordanhill College in Glasgow to train as a PE teacher. He later turned professional and joined the Light Blues on the same day that Sammy Cox arrived from Dundee. Some 48 hours later both players were in the Rangers team that played Airdrie in a Victory Cup match. Succeeding the popular Jerry Dawson, Brown's early days at Ibrox were not all sweetness and light, as the Ibrox crowd let him know what was expected of him! Brown, who had negotiated his own signing-on fee and terms, was the highest paid player at the club at this time. Yet after qualifying as a PE teacher, he took up a post at Denny High School, remaining a part-time player throughout his ten years with Rangers.

For six years—between 10 August 1946 and 16 April 1952—he never missed a League game, playing in an astonishing run of 179 matches.

Bobby Brown was to win three League Championships, three Scottish Cups in a row (1-0 in a replay against Morton in 1948, 4-1 against Clyde in 1949 and 3-0 over East Fife in 1950) and two League Cups (4-0 against Aberdeen in 1946-47 and 2-0 over Raith Rovers in 1948-49). He was also ever-present during the historic 1948-49 season, when Rangers became the first team to win the Treble.

Capped three times by Scotland, he was transferred to Falkirk in May

1956 for a fee of £2,200, but within a year he had retired and later became manager of St Johnstone, guiding them into the top division.

In February 1967, Brown was appointed manager of Scotland, a position he held until July 1971. Although Scotland failed to qualify for the 1970 World Cup, Brown had the satisfaction of a 3-2 victory over England in a European Championship qualifier at Wembley.

## JOHN BROWN

**Born:** Stirling, 26 January 1962
**Rangers career:** 1988 to 1997
**Appearances and goals:**

| League | | FA Cup | | Lg Cup | | Europe | |
|---|---|---|---|---|---|---|---|
| A | G | A | G | A | G | A | G |
| 186/21 | 14 | 29/4 | 4 | 16/2 | 0 | 17/3 | 0 |

*Total appearances:* 248/30
*Total goals:* 18
**League Championships:** 1988-89; 1989-90; 1990-91; 1991-92; 1992-93; 1993-94
**Scottish Cup:** 1991-92; 1992-93; 1995-96
**League Cup:** 1988-89; 1990-91; 1992-93

There is no diminishing the affinity the Rangers fans have for 'Bomber' Brown—he is one of them and don't they know it!

Signed in January 1988 from Dundee, he went on against all the odds—having had both cartilages removed by the time he was 15—to become one of the most popular players at the club during recent memory, a testament to his never-say-die approach to the game.

John Brown first began to catch the eye with Hamilton Academical, but it was at Dens in the mid-eighties that he first began to make a name for himself. Used as a left-back occasionally, a centre-half now and again, it was as a midfielder that Bomber was most effective for the Dark Blues. He was certainly a thorn in the side of his boyhood heroes Rangers, netting a hat-trick in a League games and netting the goal which eliminated Rangers from the Scottish Cup of 1984-85.

After a move to Hearts fell through, following the questioning of his medical record by the Tynecastle side, Brown joined Graeme Souness' Rangers side. He made his debut in a 5-0 demolition of Morton and managed to record his first goal for the club in a 3-1 win at Falkirk just a couple of matches later. However, it is not as a scorer that Brown became in-valuable for Rangers, and the utility man gradually evolved as a central defender of the highest order.

His finest season came in 1992-93, Rangers' last European campaign of any note, when Bomber, along with many other Ibrox stars, performed

*John Brown (www.snspix.com)*

heroically. His lion-hearted displays in defence brought him to the attention of many outside Scotland for the first time and prompted a number of tributes. 'In many ways he was outstanding,' Howard Wilkinson was left to reflect, after his Leeds United side had been eliminated from the European Cup by Rangers after what was dubbed the Battle of Britain.

He was the most-used player with 59 competitive appearances plus another four friendlies in that 1992-93 season, when the club went unbeaten for 44 games and progressed to within one match of the European Cup Final. He was a regular scorer for the club, famously including a goal in the New Year derby of 1992; and a rather vindictive six of his 14 league goals came against Motherwell!

His willingness to play on through the pain barrier also endeared him to the fans. In the legendary Championship decider of 1991 against Aberdeen, he opted to play despite injury problems and helped steer Rangers to the title. The day before the match he had a pain-killing injection to ensure he could train, couldn't walk on the morning of the match, still played with injections before and during the match and held the defence together until the damaged tendon ruptured altogether in the second-half. His reward? Missing much of the following season as he recovered from an operation!

Strangely, for a player who achieved so much for the Ibrox club, the closest he ever came to international recognition was a couple of calls up to squads during the 1992-93 season. But there were no caps—a shocking oversight.

John Brown is now youth coach at Ibrox, where he runs the club's reserve team, having successfully run the Under-19 side and then the Under-21s.

## TERRY BUTCHER

**Born:** Singapore, 28 December 1958
**Rangers career:** 1986 to 1990

**Appearances and goals:**

| League | | FA Cup | | Lg Cup | | Europe | |
|---|---|---|---|---|---|---|---|
| A | G | A | G | A | G | A | G |
| 127 | 8 | 11 | 0 | 21 | 0 | 17 | 2 |

*Total appearances:* 176

*Total goals:* 10

**League Championships:** 1986-87; 1988-89; 1989-90

**League Cup:** 1986-87; 1988-89

**Honours:** 77 England caps

Terry Butcher was the foundation on which the Souness Revolution was built. He was a brilliant leader and superb defender who inspired the Light Blues out of the Championship wilderness with the header that won the 1986-87 title, and if he had not suffered a broken leg in 1987-88, Rangers would have won their nine-in-a-row two seasons earlier than they did.

Born in Singapore where his father was in the Royal Navy, Butcher started out with Ipswich Town. After establishing himself as a first team regular, he won the first of 77 caps for England when he played against Australia—this after winning honours at Under-21 and 'B' international level. He helped Ipswich to a UEFA Cup Final victory over AZ Alkmaar and to runners-up spot in the First Division behind Aston Villa. He played in three consecutive World Cups, and in 1986 it was his despairing lunge that nearly prevented Maradona from scoring the greatest goal in World Cup history. Butcher, who was Town's 'Player of the Year' in 1984-85, had made 350 appearances for the Suffolk club when in August 1986 he joined Rangers for a fee of £725,000.

Butcher's signing coming so close behind that of Chris Woods, was a clear declaration to the Rangers supporters that there was fresh thinking in the club's boardroom and on the part of the management, and that the club was preparing to challenge the best teams in Europe.

His first competitive game was a 2-1 defeat against Hibs at Easter Road, a match when Graeme Souness was ordered off. Butcher though went on to have a glorious first season, leading the team to the Championship and League Cup, capping the campaign with the league-winning goal at Pittodrie.

In the Old Firm game on 17 October 1987, Butcher was ordered off with Chris Woods and Celtic's Frank McAvennie. He was all but a bystander when Woods and McAvennie played a barging game, something that goes on week in and week out in football. Butcher was booked for protesting at Woods sending-off and then booked a second time—meaning automatic dismissal—after a fairly innocuous challenge. Surprisingly the case went to court, and both Woods and Butcher were fined £250 after being found guilty of 'behaviour likely to cause a breach of the peace', while McAvennie was found not guilty! Both players took their case to the Court of Appeal but lost on a split decision.

Butcher's next appearance for Rangers resulted in him breaking his leg in the game against Aberdeen at Ibrox, a match the Dons won 1-0. On his return to action, he continued to demonstrate his good football brain, which, twinned with Richard Gough's similar abilities, started to make Rangers close to impregnable at the back. Butcher led Rangers to two more League Championships and another League Cup success before bad blood broke out between Butcher and manager Souness.

During the early stages of the 1990-91 season, Butcher was not fully fit and still recovering from his exertions of leading England to the semi-finals of the 1990 World Cup. After an error-strewn game against Dundee United, in which he scored a spectacular headed own goal, he had a row with Souness and was dropped for the Skol League Cup Final against Celtic. Butcher claimed he was injured before the game, but Souness dropped him, saying 'he has refused to play'.

Butcher was transferred to Coventry City for £440,000, taking on the role of player-manager. He spent just over a year at the helm and was forced to sack his one-time Ipswich team-mate Mick Mills, before he too lost his job when he refused to negotiate a new 'manager only' contract. The club chairman had felt he should take a cut in salary as he was suffering from a long-term injury.

Butcher later became player-manager of Sunderland, but after narrowly avoiding relegation and with the club lying bottom of the Premiership, he was sacked. During an eight-year sabbatical, Butcher ran the Old Manor Hotel in Bridge of Allan near Stirling and became a pundit for the BBC. He moved back into the game when he was appointed manager of Motherwell in 2002 and then Sydney in 2006. On the final dramatic day of the 2004-05 campaign, he led Motherwell to a 2-1 win over Celtic that enabled Rangers to clinch their 51st title with a 1-0 defeat of Hibs. On parting company with Sydney, he returned to Football League management with Brentford.

## ERIC CALDOW

**Born:** Cumnock, 14 May 1934
**Rangers career:** 1953 to 1966
**Appearances and goals:**

| League | | FA Cup | | Lg Cup | | Europe | |
|---|---|---|---|---|---|---|---|
| A | G | A | G | A | G | A | G |
| 265 | 17 | 39 | 4 | 68 | 1 | 35 | 3 |

Total appearances: 407
Total goals: 25
**League Championships:** 1955-56; 1956-57; 1958-59; 1960-61; 1962-63
**Scottish Cup:** 1959-60; 1961-62; 1962-63
**League Cup:** 1960-61; 1961-62; 1964-65
**Honours:** 40 Scotland caps

Very few men can lay claim to having played in a truly great Rangers side but full-back Eric Caldow is a rare breed—he played in two! Equally at home in either full-back berth, Caldow made his debut against Ayr United in a League Cup tie in 1953 in the company of such players as Waddell, Woodburn and Cox, and ended his Ibrox days in 1966 alongside Greig, Henderson and McKinnon.

Caldow was recommended to Rangers director George Brown by Alex Sloan, a schoolteacher friend, and on his arrival at Ibrox was farmed out to Muirkirk Juniors for a couple of seasons before being recalled in 1952. Within a year he was in the Rangers side, and by 1955-56,

*Eric Caldow (www.snspix.com)*

when the Light Blues won the League Championship, he had become a regular at right-back. But the following season, when the title was retained, he began to play more at left-back, forming a partnership with Bobby Shearer,

European football was still in its infancy when Caldow led Rangers into the first final—the Cup Winners' Cup Final of 1961—having disposed of Ferencvaros, Borussia Moenchengaldbach and Wolverhampton Wanderers, then one of the strongest teams in England, along the way. Skipper Caldow, however, was unable to lift the trophy, as Rangers lost 4-1 on aggregate to Fiorentina. In the first leg at Ibrox, Rangers were 1-0 down when they were awarded a penalty. As Caldow stepped forward to take the kick, the Italian keeper, Albertosi, ran from his goal line towards the 6-yard line gesticulating and shouting, and an astonished Caldow shot wide. Despite the protests of the Rangers players, the referee refused to allow the kick to be retaken!

He won his second winners' medals in both the Scottish Cup and League Cup in 1961-62. Hearts were beaten 3-1 in a replayed League Cup Final and St Mirren 2-0 in the Scottish FA Cup. His fifth and final League Championship medal came in 1962-63.

Captain of both Rangers and Scotland, for whom he played 40 times, Caldow won his first cap in a 4-2 victory over Spain in May 1957, and the following year played in all three of the national side's games in the World

Cup in Sweden. However, his international career was ended in horrific circumstances at Wembley in 1963—ironically when the man in front of him, Jim Baxter, secured victory for the Scots. Caldow broke his leg in three places after only six minutes of the game when tackled by Spurs and England centre-forward Bobby Smith. He had been an automatic choice for Scotland since his debut, and had missed only two games in six years. If he had been able to continue, then George Young's Rangers record of 53 caps would surely have been broken.

It took Caldow a long time to recover, and the following season he appeared in only three league games, his place at left-back being taken by Davie Provan. By 1964-65, Caldow had fought back and re-established himself in the Rangers side, winning his third League Cup winners' medal as the Light Blues beat Celtic 2-1 in the Final. But it was to be his swansong, and he played in only three games in his final season of 1965-66.

Never booked once in a long career of 407 matches for Rangers, he had a year playing for Stirling Albion before becoming player-manager of Corby Town. He was later appointed manager of Stranraer, but was not a success, and after scouting for Queen's Park Rangers, returned to Ibrox to host the new executive facilities with Alec Willoughby.

## ALFIE CONN

**Born:** Kirkcaldy, 5 April 1952
**Rangers career:** 1968 to 1974
**Appearances and goals:**

| League | | FA Cup | | Lg Cup | | Europe | |
|---|---|---|---|---|---|---|---|
| **A** | **G** | **A** | **G** | **A** | **G** | **A** | **G** |
| 78/15 | 23 | 11/2 | 3 | 23/8 | 11 | 10/2 | 2 |

*Total appearances:* 122/27
*Total goals:* 39
**Scottish Cup:** 1972-73
**League Cup:** 1970-71
**European Cup Winners Cup:** 1971-72
**Honours:** 2 Scotland caps

---

Alfie Conn was the son of a famous father of the same name, the international inside-right of the Conn-Bauld-Wardhaugh attacking trio in an excellent Hearts side of the 1940s and early 1950s.

Bursting with natural talent and confidence, the young Conn had won Scottish youth honours before signing professional forms for the Gers. He was a right-sided player with, like his father, a tremendous shot in his right foot. He played his first match for the club in Dundalk in November 1968 in what was then the 'Fairs Cities Cup'. Throughout his time at Ibrox, Conn suffered a series of niggling injuries, but it didn't prevent him from appearing in three victorious cup sides.

Conn was a natural showman with magical dribbling talents, always prepared to take a man on and beat him with pure trickery and skill. With his distinctive long curly locks flowing as defenders were left trailing in his wake, he was idolised by Rangers fans.

Having helped Rangers beat Celtic 1-0 to lift the 1970-71 League Cup, he was in Rangers' European Cup Winners Cup team, a winning team in Barcelona in 1972 as Dinamo Moscow were defeated 3-2. One of his most memorable goals was Rangers' second in their 3-2 Scottish Cup win of 1972-73, when his run on goal exposed the lack of pace of Billy McNeill, the Celtic centre-half.

In June 1974, Alfie Conn was Spurs' manager Bill Nicholson's last signing, but the £140,000 capture made just one appearance before the arrival of new manager Terry Neill. After making his debut as a substitute, Conn scored a hat-trick in a 5-2 win at Newcastle United on what was his full debut. Not helped by a number of injuries that were a direct result of his tantalising style of play, he did win two full caps for Scotland in May 1975 before finding himself languishing in Spurs' reserve side.

In March 1977 he joined Rangers' rivals Celtic on loan, with the £60,000 move made permanent after he satisfied queries about his long-term fitness. He played for the Hoops in their 1977 Scottish Cup Final success and helped them win the League Championship in both 1976-77 and 1977-78. In that 1977 Scottish Cup Final, he made history by appearing in a winning Celtic team against Rangers. Thus he had played for both Old Firm clubs against the other in winning Scottish Cup Final sides. During the following season he joined the US side Pittsburgh Spirit, and after a year moved to San Jose Earthquakes.

He then returned to Scotland to sign for Hearts. After a loan spell with Blackpool in March 1981, he joined Motherwell whom he helped win the Scottish First Division title in 1981-82. During the early part of the 1983-84 season he suffered a bad injury that forced his retirement from the game at the age of 32. He then entered management and led the Coatbridge side which won the 1985-86 Scottish Amateur Cup.

## DAVIE COOPER

**Born:** Hamilton, 25 February 1956
**Died:** Cumbernauld, 23 March 1995
**Rangers career:** 1977 to 1989
**Appearances and goals:**

| League | | FA Cup | | Lg Cup | | Europe | |
|---|---|---|---|---|---|---|---|
| A | G | A | G | A | G | A | G |
| 321/56 | 49 | 40/9 | 7 | 69/8 | 18 | 35/3 | 1 |

*Total appearances: 465/76*
*Total goals: 75*

**League Championships:** 1977-78; 1986-87; 1988-89
**Scottish Cup:** 1977-78; 1978-79; 1980-81;
**League Cup:** 1977-78; 1978-79; 1981-82; 1983-84; 1984-85; 1986-87; 1987-88
**Honours:** 22 Scotland caps

There were very few in the long history of Scottish soccer who could match the ability of 'Coop'. He possessed a left foot on a par with Jim Baxter and dazzled defenders with his stunning wing play and magnificent crosses. He also possessed tremendous shooting power that made him a scorer of spectacular goals.

As a boy, Davie Cooper was a Rangers supporter, and when he was not playing, it was to Ibrox that he went with his father and brother. Having played for local amateurs Hamilton Avondale, Cooper joined Clydebank in the summer of 1974, receiving a signing-on fee of just over £300, which was the previous night's takings from the Bankies social club! An ever-present in 1975-76, he inspired Clydebank to the Second Division title, finishing the campaign as the club's top scorer with 13 goals, including a hat-trick against Alloa Athletic. The big clubs began to take notice and Arsenal and Aston Villa tried to entice him, but Cooper was waiting for Rangers.

He got his chance to impress when Clydebank drew Rangers in the League Cup quarter-final in September 1976. It took two replays for the Light Blues to overcome Clydebank, and in the opening game, a 3-3 draw at Ibrox, Cooper scored the match-saving equaliser. At the end of that 1976-77 season, Cooper was included in the Scotland squad for the Home International Championship and the trip to South America, but immediately before he left for Chile, he signed for Rangers for a fee of £100,000.  ·

He was an instant success, appearing in 52 of Rangers 53 matches as Jock Wallace's side won the domestic treble. His first goal for Rangers came against his former club, while he saved his most important strike for the League Cup Final against Celtic, notching the first in a 2-1 win. This was to be the first of many Hampden appearances for Davie in a Rangers jersey, the stadium where, he admitted himself, he played some of his best football. His contribution to that campaign was impressive, because the club's strike duo of Derek Johnstone and Gordon Smith scored 65 goals between them. The Press, however, dubbed him 'The Moody Blue' because of his unwillingness to give interviews. Cooper was never one for the hype and preferred to do his talking on the pitch.

He won three League Championships and three Scottish Cups, scoring one of the goals in a 4-1 drubbing of Dundee United in the replayed 1981 final. The League Cup victory was his first in what became seven winners' medals in the competition, Cooper scoring four times in those seven finals.

Though he netted a hat-trick in a Sectional League Cup tie against

*In a 1982 League Cup clash, Davie Cooper races clear of Hibs' Gordon Rae*
*(www.snspix.com)*

Kilmarnock in 1982–83, it was as the scorer of some outrageous goals that he will be best remembered. In the 1979 Drybrough Cup Final against Celtic, he took the ball on his chest with his back to goal and seemingly nowhere to go. Cooper flicked the ball in the air four times with his left foot, taking him past four Celtic defenders and put it in the net. Not surprisingly it was voted the Greatest Ever Rangers Goal in a worldwide poll by fans.

He won 22 caps for Scotland and played in the 1986 World Cup Finals in Mexico, having converted one of the most famous penalties in Scottish history. It was Cooper's late spot-kick after coming off the bench that earned a draw against Wales, which to all intents and purposes took the Tartan Army to Mexico.

Cooper claimed to have been a lazy player, but when Jock Wallace returned as Rangers manager in 1983 the first words he spoke to an out-of-condition Davie Cooper were: 'You've got three weeks to lose half a stone.' The Rangers winger did it in five days! When Souness replaced Wallace as Rangers boss in 1986, the club were to win their first Championship for nine years, and it was Cooper who provided the cross for Terry Butcher to head home the goal that won the title against Aberdeen. The following season he had stopped becoming an automatic choice and joined Motherwell in search of regular first team football.

He helped Motherwell to win the Scottish Cup, beating Dundee United 4-3 after extra-time in the 1991 Final. In 1993 he returned to Clydebank as a player but also to assist in coaching duties. He was making a coaching video with Charlie Nicholas when he collapsed, dying the following day in hospital. Two of his closest friends at Ibrox—Derek Johnstone and Ally McCoist—were at his bedside when the decision was taken to switch off the life-support machine. The premature cutting down of one of the game's great entertainers sparked unprecedented mourning throughout the whole of Scotland.

## SAMMY COX

**Born:** Darvel, 13 April 1924
**Rangers career:** 1946 to 1955
**Appearances and goals:**

| League | | FA Cup | | Lg Cup | | Europe | |
|---|---|---|---|---|---|---|---|
| **A** | **G** | **A** | **G** | **A** | **G** | **A** | **G** |
| 207 | 14 | 40 | 3 | 63 | 3 | - | - |

*Total appearances:* 310
*Total goals:* 20
**League Championships:** 1946-47; 1948-49; 1949-50; 1952-53
**Scottish Cup:** 1947-48; 1948-49; 1949-50
**League Cup:** 1948-49
**Honours:** 24 Scotland caps

Sammy Cox was a versatile defender, who initially played amateur football with Queen's Park, Third Lanark and Dundee during the Second World War before turning professional in 1946, when he joined Rangers.

Having played his first game for Rangers in a 4-0 defeat of Airdrie in the Victory Cup in May 1946, he made his League debut the following August in a 4-2 win at Motherwell. He made a total of 13 appearances in his first season, including a 4-1 win over Hamilton Academical in the last match, as Rangers beat Hibernian to clinch the League title. In 1947-48, Cox was an ever-present as Rangers finished runners-up to Hibs and won the Scottish Cup with a 1-0 win over Morton.

Having appeared in a variety of positions, including right-back, right-half, left-half and inside-right, Cox moved to left-half to complete a formidable defence which also included Bobby Brown, George Young, Jock Shaw, Ian McColl and Willie Woodburn. That Iron Curtain laid the foundations for the Light Blues to become the first team to win the Treble, which they did in 1948-49. Cox, playing in 43 of Rangers' 44 matches, saw his side take the title by a point from Dundee, and beat Clyde 4-1 in the Scottish Cup and Raith Rovers 2-0 in the League Cup.

His form that season led to him winning the first of his 24 Scottish caps, when he helped his side to a 3-1 win over England at Wembley. His positional and tactical sense led him to base his defensive work on manoeuvring opponents into dead-end situations, and he had particular success against greats such as Tom Finney and Stanley Matthews. Cox captained the national side on his last appearance, also against England at Hampden Park in 1954.

Back at Ibrox, Cox was ever-present as Rangers retained the title, edging out Hibernian by one point. He also won his third and final Scottish Cup winners' medal as East Fife were beaten 3-0.

The next couple of seasons were barren years as Rangers failed to win a major honour, with Cox playing fewer games as he continually switched between left-back and left-half. But in 1952-53, Cox was back as a permanent fixture at left-half, and won the last of his three League Championship medals. But he missed out on a fourth Scottish Cup winners' medal as Rangers beat Aberdeen without him. He continued to be an important member of the Rangers side, but again found himself playing in a variety of defensive positions. He made his final Rangers appearance in a 2-1 defeat to Aberdeen in February 1955.

Cox then spent a few seasons playing for East Fife before emigrating to Canada in 1959. The quality and versatility of his positional play was such that some commentators called him a player out of his time, one they said who would have fitted naturally into the fluid Brazilian national side of the eighties.

## ALLY DAWSON

**Born:** Johnstone, 25 February 1958
**Rangers career:** 1975 to 1987
**Appearances and goals:**

| League | | FA Cup | | Lg Cup | | Europe | |
|---|---|---|---|---|---|---|---|
| **A** | **G** | **A** | **G** | **A** | **G** | **A** | **G** |
| 213/5 | 6 | 36 | 0 | 35/4 | 1 | 22/1 | 1 |

*Total appearances:* 306/10

*Total goals:* 8

**Scottish Cup:** 1978-79; 1980-81
**League Cup:** 1978-79; 1983-84; 1984-85; 1986-87
**Honours:** 5 Scotland caps

Ally Dawson joined Rangers as a 16-year-old boy during the early part of 1975, and the following summer was selected by manager Jock Wallace to go on a world tour! Dawson made his Rangers debut in Canada, showing himself to be a skilful and cultured full-back who could play on either side.

A player who liked nothing more than to get forward in support of his attack, Dawson scored his first goal for the club in a 2-1 win at Dundee United during the 1978-79 season. That season he was a member of the Rangers sides that won both the Scottish Cup, beating Hibernian 3-2 after two goalless drawn games, and the League Cup, following a 2-1 defeat of Aberdeen.

Though he was appointed Rangers' club captain, he never quite became the wholly exceptional player everyone expected him to be, because of a serious injury he sustained on a club tour of Canada in 1980 when he fractured his skull.

He missed the first half of the 1980-81 season, but returned to the side at left-back and won the first of five full international caps for Scotland, and picked up his second Scottish Cup winners' medal in another replayed final, as Rangers beat Dundee United 4-1 at the second attempt.

Dawson won further League Cup winners' medals in 1983-84 and 1984-85 as Celtic and Dundee United were beaten 3-2 and 1-0 respectively. By the time he picked up his fourth and final League Cup winners' medal in 1986-87, Dawson had become a poised, neatly balanced central defender, helping Rangers beat their great rivals Celtic 2-1 at Hampden Park.

Ally Dawson was a great servant to Rangers Football Club, and had appeared in 316 League and Cup games before he left Ibrox and joined Blackburn Rovers in a £25,000 move in the summer of 1987.

Dawson spent a couple of seasons at Ewood Park, but unfortunately most of his time with the Lancashire club was spent on the treatment table as he suffered a spate of niggling injuries. Unable to hold down a regular place in the Ewood Park club's side, he returned north of the border and joined Airdrie. But sadly, once again injuries hampered his progress and he was forced into premature retirement.

## BILLY DODDS

**Born:** New Cumnock, 5 February 1969
**Rangers career:** 1999 to 2002
**Appearances and goals:**

| League | | FA Cup | | Lg Cup | | Europe | |
|---|---|---|---|---|---|---|---|
| **A** | **G** | **A** | **G** | **A** | **G** | **A** | **G** |
| 38/27 | 21 | 3/4 | 9 | 2/1 | 1 | 3/6 | 3 |

*Total appearances:* 46/38
*Total goals:* 34
**League Championships:** 1999-2000
**Scottish Cup:** 1999-2000; 2001-02

Much-travelled striker Billy Dodds has always been something of a cult figure to the fans of the clubs he has played for. Even on occasions where Dodds has not been in particularly good form, his ability to perform a piece of fantastic football from a seemingly hopeless situation has always made him a popular figure.

He first appeared on the books of Chelsea, but had his first taste of professional football in a successful loan period with Partick Thistle in 1987-88. He returned to Chelsea, but after making only two appearances for the Stamford Bridge club, he was transferred to Dundee in 1989 where he became a most prolific striker. He was the club's leading scorer in the majority of his seasons at Dens Park, helping them win the First Division Championship in 1991-92 when he topped the scoring charts with 19 goals.

After a spell with St Johnstone, who paid £300,000 for his services, Dodds moved to Aberdeen where he was part of the side that won the League Cup in 1996, beating his former club Dundee 2-0 in the final. It was while at Pittodrie, that Dodds won the first of his 26 Scottish caps when he played against Latvia in a World Cup qualifier in Latvia. He then moved to Dundee United for his first spell at Tannadice and began attracting the attention of Scotland coach Craig Brown, who restored Dodds to the Scotland squad after a 12-month absence. His Tannadice career got off to a flying start with a hat-trick on his first start against former club St Johnstone.

It was in December 1999 that Billy Dodds made the biggest move of his career in a surprise £1.3 million swoop by the then manager of Rangers, Dick Advocaat. Dodds proved an instant success at Ibrox, scoring goals domestically and in European competition. He scored twice in a 5-1 win at Motherwell, going on to score 10 goals in 16 starts as the Gers won the League Championship and netted a hat-trick in a 7-0 League Cup semi-final defeat of Ayr United before scoring in the final as Aberdeen were beaten 4-0.

He started the 2000-01 season in fine style, scoring seven goals in the first five games but then injuries and a loss of form cost him his place in the side. He was a member of the Rangers side that completed the Scottish and League Cup double the following season, helping the club on their way in the latter tournament with a hat-trick in a 6-0 rout of Forfar Athletic. In December 2002, frustrated by the lack of first team chances under new Rangers boss Alex McLeish, Dodds returned to Dundee United in a deal that saw Steven Thompson move in the opposite direction.

Dodds relished the opportunity of playing football on a regular basis and became a key member of the Dundee United side. Appointed the club's player-coach, he took over as caretaker manager for one match following the sacking of Gordon Chisholm. However, following the appointment of Craig Brewster, Dodds parted company with the club and had a brief spell with Partick Thistle before working as an analyst/commentator on BBC Radio Scotland.

## JIMMY DUNCANSON

**Born:** Glasgow, 13 October 1919
**Died:** Glasgow, 1 January 1996
**Rangers career:** 1946 to 1950
**Appearances and goals:**

| League | | FA Cup | | Lg Cup | | Europe | |
|---|---|---|---|---|---|---|---|
| A | G | A | G | A | G | A | G |
| 93 | 41 | 17 | 7 | 30 | 11 | - | - |

*Total appearances:* 140
*Total goals:* 59
**League Championships:** 1946-47; 1948-49
**Scottish Cup:** 1947-48; 1948-49; 1949-50
**League Cup:** 1946-47; 1948-49
**Honours:** 1 Scotland cap

An aggressive striker, red-haired Jimmy Duncanson joined Rangers in 1939, but had to wait until after the Second World War to realise his vast potential. An inside-left in the mould of his pre-war predecessor Bob McPhail, Duncanson's greatest single talent was probably his ability to find the net in Old Firm matches!

Having scored 77 goals in wartime fixtures for the Light Blues, in 1946-47 he was joint-top scorer in the League with Willie Thornton, both players netting a total of 18 times, with Duncanson hitting a hat-trick in a 4-0 home win over St Mirren. As well as winning the League Championship, Rangers also won the League Cup, with Duncanson netting twice in the final as Aberdeen were beaten 4-0. His form in that first post-war season saw him win his only full international cap for Scotland, although he had appeared in a couple of wartime internationals.

Though the game against Northern Ireland at Hampden was goalless, Duncanson hit the post and laid on goalscoring chances for Rangers' team-mate Willie Thornton and Liverpool legend Billy Liddell.

Quick and combative, the strike force he formed with Thornton was the most deadly in the Scottish League at this time, and in 1947-48, though Rangers had to be content with the runners-up spot in the League, Duncanson continued to find the net and hit all three goals in a 3-1 win at Dundee on Christmas Day 1947. Included in that treble was the club's 4000th goal.

In 1948-49, Duncanson was an important member of the club's treble-winning team, and his hat-trick against Celtic in the Ne'erday game was the first by a Rangers player in an Old Firm Scottish League fixture in the 20th century! In fact, Duncanson's total of 22 goals in games against the Hoops is bettered by only two players in the club's history—RC Hamilton and Ally McCoist. Also that season, Duncanson scored in the Scottish Cup Final as Clyde were well beaten 4-0.

In November 1950, Duncanson was surprisingly allowed to join St Mirren. He continued to find the net on a regular basis at Love Street before moving to Stranraer, where he ended his playing days after a couple of seasons at Stair Park.

Jimmy Duncanson remained a fervent Rangers supporter, and in his later days was often seen watching his beloved team from the terraces at Ibrox.

## GORDON DURIE

**Born:** Paisley, 6 December 1965
**Rangers career:** 1993 to 1999
**Appearances and goals:**

| League | | FA Cup | | Lg Cup | | Europe | |
|---|---|---|---|---|---|---|---|
| **A** | **G** | **A** | **G** | **A** | **G** | **A** | **G** |
| 90/35 | 43 | 17/2 | 9 | 7/3 | 2 | 18/7 | 5 |

*Total appearances:* 132/47
*Total goals:* 59
**League Championships:** 1993-94; 1994-95; 1995-96; 1996-97
**Scottish Cup:** 1995-96
**League Cup:** 1998-99
**Honours:** 43 Scotland caps

A skilful, strong-running striker, the most successful period of Gordon Durie's career came while playing for Rangers, where he was part of the nine-in-a-row winning side of 1996-97.

He began his career with Scottish junior side Hill o' Beath before signing for East Fife and later Hibernian. It was at Easter Road that he first made his mark on the game, attracting scouts from south of the border. Chelsea moved in quickly for him, and though at first he found it difficult to hold down a regular place, once David Speedie had left for Coventry City, he became a regular up front alongside England international Kerry Dixon. Although his time at Stamford Bridge was hampered by injuries, he still managed to score 62 goals in 152 games, including five in a 7-0 win at Walsall during 1988-89, a season in which Chelsea ran away with the Second Division Championship.

While with Chelsea, Durie won the first of his 43 international caps for Scotland when he came off the bench in the European Championship qualifier against Bulgaria. His performances for the national side over the years have been enough to earn Durie a silver medal from the SFA in their Hall of Fame scheme. Certainly not prolific at international level, his strikes against

*Gordon Durie*

San Marino and Switzerland in Scotland's unlikely qualification for the 1992 European Championship were vital.

Prior to the start of the 1991-92 season, Durie was transferred to Tottenham Hotspur for a massive fee, and compared to his time at Chelsea, he remained relatively injury-free at White Hart Lane. Though at first his goalscoring touch deserted him, he bounced back with a hat-trick against Coventry City. Even so, his time at the North London club was not successful, with a 'cheating' charge, although eventually dismissed, hanging over him. He also had a very public bust-up with boss Ossie Ardiles over a substitution he did not agree with.

Durie joined Rangers in the run-in to the 1993-94 league season, proving a worthwhile acquisition by ending the season as the Light Blues second-top-scorer with 12 Premier Division goals. There was no doubting Walter Smith's delight as Durie earned his first major medal in the game. Rangers won the title for a seventh successive season in 1994-95, with Durie netting one of the goals that secured the Championship in a 3-1 defeat of Hibs.

Gordon Durie's greatest performance in a Rangers shirt came in the 1996 Scottish Cup Final against Hearts when he netted a hat-trick in a 5-1 win. It was the first Cup Final hat-trick since Dixie Deans managed the feat for Celtic against Hibs in 1972. Despite Durie's treble, the game is always remembered as Laudrup's final, for as well as setting up Durie, he scored twice himself! Durie also managed 17 league goals, including a hat-trick in a 4-0 win at Partick Thistle and four in a 7-0 rout of Hibs.

After that, 'Jukebox', as he was known, began to suffer with a number of niggling injuries, and, after his appearances became less frequent, he decided to call time on his playing days.

## IAN DURRANT

**Born:** Glasgow, 29 September 1966
**Rangers career:** 1983 to 1998

**Appearances and goals:**

| League | | FA Cup | | Lg Cup | | Europe | |
|---|---|---|---|---|---|---|---|
| *A* | *G* | *A* | *G* | *A* | *G* | *A* | *G* |
| 193/56 | 26 | 10/9 | 3 | 37/3 | 8 | 28/11 | 8 |

*Total appearances:* 268/79
*Total goals:* 45
**League Championships:** 1986-87; 1992-93; 1993-94; 1994-95
**Scottish Cup:** 1991-92; 1992-93; 1995-96
**League Cup:** 1986-87; 1987-88; 1992-93; 1993-94
**Honours:** 20 Scotland caps

---

Ian Durrant possessed a prodigious talent and enjoyed a tremendous career with the Ibrox club. But it could have been so much better had it not been for Neil Simpson's horrendous challenge in 1988, which put him out of the game for almost three years.

The Light Blues were Ian Durrant's boyhood team, and he joined his heroes while still at school. After working his way up through the ranks, he made his debut against Morton in April 1985, and the following season established himself as a permanent fixture in the Rangers side, scoring his first goal for the club in his debut Old Firm game at Ibrox. The arrival of Graeme Souness at the club meant that Durrant would have sole use of the No.10 shirt throughout the whole of the 1986-87 season.

Over the course of that campaign, Durrant appeared in 39 games as Rangers won the Championship. The Light Blues also won the League Cup, beating Celtic 2-1, with Durrant scoring his side's opening goal. Rangers retained the League Cup the following season in one of the great finals of the modern era. Rangers and their opponents Aberdeen were level at 2-2 after ninety minutes, and when extra-time saw no further breakthrough, the game went to penalties. It was Durrant's spot-kick that decided the tie and he stood, arms aloft in that famous 'Victory V' salute!

Almost exactly a year later, tragedy struck at Pittodrie when a wild challenge by Aberdeen's Neil Simpson left the Rangers midfielder with a shattered knee. The fact that an out-of-court settlement was reached for compensation was proof enough of its recklessness. Durrant was aged just 21 and had already made 122 appearances for the Ibrox club.

He made his return in April 1991 in a reserve team fixture against Hibernian, and was welcomed back by a crowd of 35,000. His return to the Rangers team coincided with extraordinary success for both club and player in the 1992-93 season with a domestic treble and unqualified success in Europe, including Durrant's memorable strike to quieten the fanatical supporters of Marseille during the European campaign. He was instrumental in the club's 44-game unbeaten run before forcing his way back into the Scotland set-up.

Durrant went on to win four League Championship medals, four League

*In a 1992 European tie, Ian Durrant takes the ball away from Gordon Strachan of Leeds (www.snspix.com)*

Cup winners' medals, including scoring in the 1993-94 final against Hibs, and three Scottish Cup winners' medals. Shortly after these successes, questions were being asked about Durrant's fitness and he was loaned out to Everton. He impressed in his stay at Goodison Park, but returned to Scotland after the Ibrox club were reluctant to release him. Yet it seemed that he did not have the fitness required to play football week-in, week-out. Also, his misfortune was compounded in that he was being asked to play in an alien way to his natural style, because the Scottish League could not be tailored to his skilful talents.

In 1998, along with fellow Rangers team-mate Ally McCoist, Durrant transferred to Kilmarnock, where his form led to him winning another recall to Scotland's colours. He spent two seasons at Rugby Park, but an injury in the CIS Cup Final against Celtic, which Killie lost 3-0, kept him out of action for 14 months until he came off the bench as a late substitute against Dundee United in May 2002, basically to say farewell to the fans.

On hanging up his boots, he became Kilmarnock's youth team coach, but in 2005 returned to Rangers as coach of the Under-19s and later the reserve team. Following the resignation of Paul le Guen as Rangers manager in January 2007, Durrant was temporarily elevated to the position of manager at Ibrox until Walter Smith was re-appointed.

## BARRY FERGUSON

**Born:** Glasgow, 2 February 1978
**Rangers career:** 1994 to 2003 and 2005 to present
**Appearances and goals:**

| League | | FA Cup | | Lg Cup | | Europe | |
|---|---|---|---|---|---|---|---|
| A | G | A | G | A | G | A | G |
| 223/3 | 38 | 26/2 | 6 | 17/2 | 3 | 63/1 | 5 |

*Total appearances:* 329/8
*Total goals:* 52
**League Championships:** 1998-99; 1999-2000; 2002-03; 2004-05
**Scottish Cup:** 1999-2000; 2002-03
**League Cup:** 1998-99; 2001-02; 2002-03; 2004-05
**Honours:** 39 Scotland caps

Currently captain of both Rangers and the Scotland national team, midfielder Barry Ferguson arrived at Ibrox at the age of 13 and joined the groundstaff—cleaning boots while impressing in both schoolboy and youth team games. Rising through the ranks of one of Scotland's biggest clubs, he went on to be one of the more successful products of Rangers' youth system.

Ferguson was voted Man-of-the-Match on his debut appearance for Rangers against Hearts on the final day of the 1996-97 season, and scored his first league goal for the Light Blues the following September in a 2-0 win over Dunfermline Athletic. He became a permanent first team fixture in the 1998-99 season under new manager Dick Advocaat. Ferguson grew into a high quality, skilful midfielder and was soon noticed by the Scottish FA, making his international debut for Scotland in a European Championship qualifier against Lithuania.

He soon became the club's youngest-ever captain of the team, and in 2001-02, guided Rangers to a League Cup and Scottish Cup double. That was also the first season in charge for Alex McLeish, and in 2002-03, their second season together, Ferguson captained the side to a domestic treble. He

*Rangers captain Barry Ferguson celebrates a 2-0 win over Old Firm rivals Celtic in 2007 (www.snspix.com)*

also won the Scottish Football Writers' Association Footballer of the Year award and Scottish PFA's Player of the Year. Also that season, he netted all three goals in a 3-0 defeat of Dundee United—his first hat-trick for the club.

The midfielder signed new long-term deals on many occasions with the club, but his ambition and desire for new challenges became too much, and after that successful treble-winning season, he handed in a transfer request. After 35 goals in 231 appearances for the Gers, Ferguson joined his former Rangers team-mate Lorenzo Amoruso at Ewood Park.

He certainly didn't have an easy time of it in England, and struggled to settle at Blackburn, with homesickness and the team's poor form hitting him hard. Excited by the thought of playing in the Premiership, he played in virtually every game—including scoring in a 4-0 victory at Birmingham City, which seemed to be a turning point in the club's fortunes—until the Christmas clash with Newcastle United. Ferguson then broke his kneecap following an innocuous challenge from Gary Speed, and did not feature again in 2003-04.

In the close season, Graeme Souness made Ferguson captain of Blackburn and he seemed to be adapting very well to Premiership football, despite the team still struggling and a managerial change which saw Mark Hughes replace Souness. However, in January 2005 he handed in a transfer request to try and force a move back to Rangers. Finally, with one hour left in the transfer window, the £4.5 million deal was struck and he moved back to Glasgow.

His first game back was a 7-1 drubbing of Dundee United in the League Cup. He continued to be an important member of the team which won the SPL in dramatic style, scoring twice in 15 games, though he was sent off in the game with Motherwell! He was not captain for this match, however, with McLeish not wanting to remove the leadership mid-season from Fernando Ricksen. Ferguson was re-appointed captain for 2005-06, although he played the last part of the campaign carrying an injury. This was later to be revealed as snapped ligaments, and he confessed that he should have undergone the surgery sooner.

In June 2006, Ferguson was awarded the MBE, and is the only current Rangers player to be inducted into the club's Hall of Fame.

On New Year's Day 2007, it was announced that Ferguson had been stripped of the captaincy after a meeting with Paul le Guen. He was also dropped from the squad, with Le Guen later claiming he was undermining him. Rangers won the match at Motherwell 1-0 with striker Kris Boyd holding up six fingers—Ferguson's shirt number—reportedly showing solidarity with the deposed skipper. Following the resignation of Le Guen and the re-appointment of Walter Smith, Ferguson was immediately re-instated as captain.

## IAN FERGUSON

**Born:** Glasgow, 15 March 1967
**Rangers career:** 1988 to 2000
**Appearances and goals:**

| League | | FA Cup | | Lg Cup | | Europe | |
|---|---|---|---|---|---|---|---|
| **A** | **G** | **A** | **G** | **A** | **G** | **A** | **G** |
| 204/33 | 24 | 26/1 | 6 | 23/8 | 8 | 32/7 | 4 |

*Total appearances: 285/49*
*Total goals: 42*
**League Championships:** 1988-89; 1989-90; 1990-91; 1991-92; 1992-93; 1993-94;
    1994-95; 1995-96; 1996-97; 1998-99
**Scottish Cup:** 1992-93; 1995-96; 1998-99
**League Cup:** 1988-89; 1990-91; 1992-93; 1993-94; 1998-99
**Honours:** 9 Scotland caps

Ian Ferguson is one of only three players, along with Ally McCoist and Richard Gough, who was talented, durable and lucky enough to win a

Championship Badge in each of Rangers historic nine-in-a-row titles during the 1990s. Maybe his large medal collection is Lady Luck's way of repaying Fergie for the grim determination he showed in 1988, when he repeatedly insisted he wanted to leave St Mirren and join Rangers, although the £1 million deal took an interminable time to be agreed.

When he first burst onto the scene with Clyde in 1985-86, he was already earmarked as a star in the making before Alex Smith at St Mirren was impressed enough to take the budding star to Paisley in 1986. It was a move the Buddies were to be grateful for many times over, when towards the end of the 1986-87 season, it seemed that the whole of Renfrewshire was at Hampden Park to see them beat Dundee United 1-0 in the Scottish Cup Final. After a dull ninety minutes, it was Ferguson, then only 20 years old, who crashed home the winner for the club's first silverware in 37 years!

His first season at Ibrox was a vintage one for the midfielder, scoring in a 4-1 defeat of Celtic, an overhead goal in the 3-2 League Cup Final win against Aberdeen and a vicious free-kick at Parkhead for Rangers' first victory there for nine years. Unfortunately, he then missed a number of matches over the next couple of seasons through illness and injury, but returned to score the vital winner against CSKA Moscow during Rangers spectacular 1992-93 European Champions' League run. The following season he held the Rangers' midfield together at a time when the club was in the grip of an injury crisis, appearing in more matches than anyone else.

Yet for all his success—10 League Championships, five League Cup winners' medals and three Scottish Cup winners' medals, Ferguson has had his low spots. In 1993-94, the temperamental Ferguson was red-carded for spitting against Gordon Petric of Dundee United. Despite the fact that the Yugoslavian had clearly elbowed the Rangers man, the furore was massive. Players like Victor Ferreyra of United and St Mirren's Chic Charnley had been booted out of their clubs for the same misdemeanour. There were calls for him to be kicked out of Ibrox but Walter Smith's commonsense prevailed and the punishment was kept within the walls of the club—although the SFA hammered the errant Ferguson with a lengthy match ban. After 'doing his time', he was soon back to his best, charging forward and winning balls in the centre of the park.

The only real blight in Ferguson's career was his lamentable international record, which frustrated both Andy Roxburgh and Craig Brown. Following his debut against Italy back in 1988, Ferguson withdrew from numerous squads for a variety of injuries!

Ferguson was a regular at Ibrox under Graeme Souness and then Walter Smith, but rarely played under Dick Advocaat and moved on to Dunfermline Athletic in 2000. He helped the Pars avoid relegation in the two seasons he was there, but just before the start of the 2002-03 season, he surprisingly emigrated to Australia to play for Northern Spirit FC as Rangers had established a major stake in the club. More recently he has played and been made head coach of the Central Coast Mariners in New South Wales, who play in the Australian A-League.

## WILLIE FINDLAY

**Born:** Motherwell, 15 November 1926
**Died:** 9 January 2001
**Rangers career:** 1947 to 1954
**Appearances and goals:**

| League | | FA Cup | | Lg Cup | | Europe | |
|---|---|---|---|---|---|---|---|
| **A** | **G** | **A** | **G** | **A** | **G** | **A** | **G** |
| 70 | 37 | 11 | 7 | 33 | 21 | | |

*Total appearances:* 114
*Total goals:* 65
**League Championships:** 1949-50
**Scottish Cup:** 1949-50

Willie Findlay's entire desire seemed to be to score goals, and during his time with Rangers, he had a talent for finding good scoring positions in the penalty area.

Findlay started out with Albion Rovers, having played junior football for Blantyre Victoria prior to signing for his new club in 1941. He quickly formed a successful right-wing partnership with Rovers' established favourite Johnny McIlhatton. The talented newcomer quickly endeared himself to the Rovers' fans by playing a major role in a 4-3 win, after being three goals down, over Airdrie on Ne'erday 1942.

Lanky and unassuming, Findlay joined Rangers for a fee of £7,500 in April 1947, but had to wait until the following season before making a scoring debut in an Old Firm match which Rangers won 2-0. Three games later he netted a brace in a 3-0 win at Queen of the South, but then lost out until the last couple of games of the campaign, which he finished with six goals in seven outings.

In 1948-49, Findlay made 12 appearances as Rangers won the Division One Championship, but the following season as the Gers repeated the achievement, Findlay started the campaign with a goal on the opening day of the season in a 2-0 defeat of Partick Thistle, and four scored in the first five games. That season, Rangers also reached the Scottish Cup Final where their opponents were East Fife. Within thirty seconds of the kick-off, Eddie Rutherford crossed and the ever-alert Willie Findlay scored with a diving header from 18 yards. East Fife came back strongly, but two goals from Willie Thornton, both of which the irrepressible Findlay had a hand in, helped Rangers to a 3-0 success.

He was known as 'Banana Findlay', because every pass he played seemed to have a 'bend' on it. Not the greatest worker Rangers ever had, he was however a keen and persistent penalty area player, and in March 1951, he netted his first hat-trick for the club in a 5-2 home win over Falkirk.

Findlay netted another treble on the opening day of the following season as Partick Thistle were beaten 4-1 at Ibrox. That 1951-52 season saw Rangers reach the League Cup Final, but despite Findlay getting on the scoresheet, the Light Blues went down 3-2 to Dundee.

Though Findlay was not a physical player, he could snap up defensive blunders without fear. He served Willie Waddell well on the wing, and yet always seemed to be on hand when the Waddell crosses came in. Having scored 65 goals in 114 League and Cup games and won League Championship and Scottish Cup medals, Findlay found his first team place coming under threat, and midway through the 1954-55 season, he left Ibrox to rejoin his first club Albion Rovers on a free transfer.

## JIM FORREST

**Born:** Glasgow, 22 September 1944
**Rangers career:** 1962 to 1967
**Appearances and goals:**

| League | | FA Cup | | Lg Cup | | Europe | |
|---|---|---|---|---|---|---|---|
| A | G | A | G | A | G | A | G |
| 105 | 83 | 10 | 6 | 37 | 50 | 11 | 6 |

*Total appearances:* 163
*Total goals:* 145
**League Championships:** 1963-64
**League Cup:** 1963-64; 1964-65
**Honours:** 5 Scotland caps

One of the Scottish League's greatest-ever goalscorers, as his goals-to-games played ratio testifies, Jim Forrest was the ideal centre-forward. Though he was occasionally criticised for being nothing more than a goalscorer, he combined unselfishly with his team-mates and held an attacking line together well.

Forrest joined the Ibrox club as a schoolboy, but was sent briefly to play for Drumchapel Amateurs to aid his development before making his Rangers debut in a 4-0 home win over Falkirk in November 1962. The following season, Forrest established himself as an important member of the Rangers side, helping them win the League Championship and the League Cup. Forrest's total of 21 league goals in 24 games included a hat-trick in a 3-0 victory at Partick Thistle followed by four goals in a 5-0 away win at Third Lanark a couple of weeks later. Having netted four goals in an early round of the League Cup as Queen of the South were beaten 5-2, Forrest repeated the feat in the Final—his cousin, Alex Willoughby got the other goal—as Rangers' opponents, Morton, were well beaten 5-0.

One of a handful of players since the Second World War to have scored a hundred League goals, Jim Forrest had a most memorable 1964-65 season. He netted 57 goals in all competitions that season, including 30 goals in 30 games in the League. That total included two hauls of four goals in a game, as St Mirren were beaten 7-0 at Love Street and Falkirk 6-1 at Ibrox. He also netted a couple of hat-tricks in a 9-2 victory over Airdrie and a 4-0 defeat of Dundee. That season, he scored 18 goals in the club's run to yet another League Cup Final, including another four as St Johnstone were demolished 9-1, and both goals in the Final, as Rangers retained the trophy with a 2-1 defeat of arch-rivals Celtic.

That 1964-65 season saw Rangers enjoy a European Cup run that saw aggregate triumphs over Red Star Belgrade and Rapid Vienna. The victory over Red Star was a drawn-out affair, and with the scores level after two legs, Highbury was chosen as a neutral venue. Forrest found the English ground very much to his liking, scoring twice in a 3-1 win, having already scored in the first game at Ibrox. Another goal in the win over Rapid Vienna meant he was full of confidence as Rangers met Inter Milan in the quarter-finals. Only 19-years-old, Forrest scored in the 3-1 first leg defeat in Italy and then netted Gers' winning goal in the second leg at Ibrox. Though George McLean later hit a post, the Light Blues lost 3-2 on aggregate against a team that went on to win the World Club Championship as well as the European Cup that year.

During the 1965-66 season, in which Rangers finished as runners-up to Celtic, Jim Forrest went one better by scoring five goals in a 7-1 win at Hamilton Academical. He also scored 10 goals in 10 games in the League Cup as Rangers reached their third successive Final, where they went down 2-1 to Celtic. Jim Forrest's Ibrox career ended under the cloud of the infamous Scottish Cup defeat by Berwick Rangers in January 1967.

Unbelievably blamed for this surprise reversal, he was transfer-listed and within weeks had joined Preston North End. Though he scored on his debut, he struggled throughout the 1967-68 campaign and returned north to play for Aberdeen, helping the Pittodrie club win the 1970 Scottish Cup Final. He left the Dons in 1973 to see out his career with Hong Kong Rangers.

## TOM FORSYTH

**Born:** Glasgow, 23 January 1949
**Rangers career:** 1972 to 1982
**Appearances and goals:**

| League | | FA Cup | | Lg Cup | | Europe | |
|---|---|---|---|---|---|---|---|
| **A** | **G** | **A** | **G** | **A** | **G** | **A** | **G** |
| 213/7 | 1 | 36 | 2 | 50 | 2 | 22/1 | 0 |

*Total appearances:* 321/8
*Total goals:* 5

**League Championships:** 1974-75; 1975-76; 1977-78
**Scottish Cup:** 1972-73; 1975-76; 1977-78; 1980-81
**League Cup:** 1975-76; 1977-78
**Honours:** 22 Scotland caps

Nicknamed 'Jaws' by sportswriter Allan Heron for his uncompromising style of play and ferocious tackling, Tom Forsyth started out as a midfield player and famously scored the winner from just six inches out in the 1973 Scottish Cup Final against Celtic, after Derek Johnstone's header had struck a post and rolled invitingly along the line!

Forsyth started his career with Motherwell, which he joined from Stonehouse Violet in 1967, playing the majority of his 150 games at Fir Park at inside-forward or wing-half. In fact, his displays for the Steelmen led to him winning the first of his 22 full international caps for Scotland against Denmark.

In October 1972, Forsyth joined Rangers for a fee of £40,000 and made his debut against his old club Motherwell in a match Rangers won 2-0. It was Rangers' boss Jock Wallace who converted Forsyth into the complete defender. Though he rarely ventured forward, he did score his only league goals during the course of Rangers' League Championship-winning season of 1974-75 as Morton were beaten 2-0.

He was part of the Rangers' treble-winning side of 1975-76, going on to win three League Championship medals, four Scottish Cup winners' medals and three League Cup winners' medals.

At international level, Forsyth was a stalwart at the heart of the national side's defence, although Tommy Docherty once famously labelled him 'a carthorse'. Ally MacLeod had much more faith in him, and he played in all three Scotland games in the 1978 World Cup Finals in Argentina. Forsyth, who played in 22 internationals, had the honour of captaining the side in only his third appearance at this level as Switzerland were beaten 1-0.

Forsyth made the last of his 329 League and Cup appearances in a 4-1 win over St Mirren in November 1981, and was out of action for four months before later being forced to retire through injury. In the autumn of 1982, Forsyth was appointed manager of Dunfermline Athletic, but having formed a close affinity and friendship with Tom McLean while at Ibrox, he relinquished his post and joined him as his assistant at his former club Motherwell. When McLean moved to Hearts, Tom Forsyth went with him to Tynecastle, but it proved to be his last post in senior Scottish football.

Tom Forsyth is now working as a Match Day host at his beloved Ibrox most weekends.

# PAUL GASCOIGNE

**Born:** Gateshead, 27 May 1967
**Rangers career:** 1995 to 1998
**Appearances and goals:**

| League | | FA Cup | | Lg Cup | | Europe | |
|---|---|---|---|---|---|---|---|
| **A** | **G** | **A** | **G** | **A** | **G** | **A** | **G** |
| 64/9 | 30 | 7/1 | 3 | 7 | 4 | 15 | 2 |

*Total appearances:* 93/10
*Total goals:* 39
**League Championships:** 1995-96; 1996-97
**Scottish Cup:** 1995-96
**League Cup:** 1996-97
**Honours:** 57 England caps

There were those who questioned the signing of Paul Gascoigne. The England international had a history of injuries, on-field disciplinary problems and off-field skirmishes, and there was also a feeling that he was past his best. Though his behaviour problems persisted at Ibrox, the quality of his play was wonderful, often as good as anyone who had ever donned the light blue jersey.

Gascoigne progressed through the ranks at Newcastle United to make his League debut a month before turning professional. Quickly establishing himself as the most exciting talent of his generation, he was voted 'Young Player of the Year' by the PFA in 1988. His sense of humour got him into trouble, but after scoring 25 goals in 107 games for the Magpies, Spurs manager Terry Venables signed Gazza for a British record fee of £2 million. Within 11 days of his Spurs debut at Newcastle, when the Geordie fans pelted him with Mars bars, he won his first full England cap when he came off the bench against Denmark.

He was hailed as the player around whom England should build its team for the 1990 World Cup. His televised tears when he realised his booking in the semi-final would rule him out of the final, were England to progress, endeared him to football fans everywhere.

After the World Cup, Gascoigne carried on where he had left off, steering Spurs almost single-handedly to the 1991 FA Cup Final. His day was ruined after only 15 minutes by a serious ligament injury caused by a rash challenge on his part, and he was carried off. The career-threatening damage to his cruciate ligament put his record £8.5 million move to Lazio in jeopardy, but after taking a year to recover, he eventually moved for £5 million to show the Italians what he could do.

Gascoigne was 28 when he joined Rangers and scored on his home debut in a 4-0 victory over Steaua Bucharest in the Ibrox International Trophy in July 1995. By only his fourth League match for the Gers, he had catapulted himself into the club's folklore with a stunning goal in a 2-0 victory over

*Paul Gascoigne in action against Aberdeen in 1996 (www.snspix.com)*

Celtic. It was a magnificent example of what he could do, but his most important contribution in his first season with the club came when the chips were down. Rangers were facing Aberdeen and victory would give them their eighth successive League title.

The Dons were leading 1-0 when Gascoigne went past two defenders and from the narrowest of angles chipped the keeper for the equalising goal. He followed this by getting possession in his own half and running 50 yards, his strength and determination seeing off a couple of challenges, before placing the ball in the far corner of the goal. Then he sealed his hat-trick and the Championship with a penalty. It was a one-man show! He also picked up a Scottish Cup winners' medal that season as Rangers beat Hearts 5-1.

The other side of the coin was Paul Gascoigne's disciplinary record. During the 7-0 drubbing of Hibernian in December 1995, referee Doug Smith dropped his yellow card, which was picked up by Gascoigne and waved at the official in a mock caution. The referee didn't see the funny side and booked the Rangers midfielder! However, by the time he was shown the yellow card in the drawn Old Firm game with Celtic in March 1996, he had been booked in five consecutive League games, and it was his 16th caution in 32 games.

After his second full season, Gascoigne had played in nine Old Firm games, winning seven, never losing and scoring a couple of goals and making a couple. Yet as his personal problems away from the pitch continued to attract publicity, Walter Smith went into print towards the end of the 1996-97 season to admit that Gazza's behaviour had often led him to question seriously whether he had been right to make the £4.3 million signing from Lazio.

His injury jinx struck again in January 1997 against Ajax and he was out of action for three months, returning to fitness in time to help win the Nine in a Row. He won a League Cup winners' medal in the 4-3 victory over Hearts, scoring twice, having already netted a hat-trick in a 5-0 League victory over Motherwell. Midway through the following season, with speculation rife that Gascoigne was on his way south, he signed for Middlesbrough for £3.5 million.

One of the most gifted players ever to wear the Rangers jersey, he was adored by the Ibrox fans.

With Boro, he became the first player to make his debut for a club in a Wembley Cup Final when he came off the bench in the League Cup Final against Chelsea. His charisma on and off the pitch led to Boro's late successful promotion bid to the Premiership, but he was not part of England's World Cup '98 squad following a well-documented argument with manager Glenn Hoddle. On leaving Teeside, he had spells with Everton and Burnley, before the next twist in his career took him to China and and a brief foray into management with Kettering Town.

# TORRY GILLICK

**Born:** Airdrie, 19 May 1915
**Died:** 12 December 1971
**Rangers career:** 1946 to 1950
**Appearances and goals:**

| League | | FA Cup | | Lg Cup | | Europe | |
|---|---|---|---|---|---|---|---|
| A | G | A | G | A | G | A | G |
| 104 | 49 | 16 | 5 | 20 | 8 | - | - |

*Total appearances:* 140
*Total goals:* 62
**League Championships:** 1946-47
**Scottish Cup:** 1934-35; 1947-48
**League Cup:** 1946-47; 1948-49
**Honours:** 5 Scotland caps

A supremely skilful inside-forward, Torry Gillick was unique in that he was the only player that Rangers' fabled boss Bill Struth welcomed back to Ibrox a second time, after he had left the club.

At the age of 15, Gillick was playing for one of Glasgow's most prominent junior clubs, Petershill. Rangers signed him in 1933 before he was 18 as a winger, and he won a Scottish Cup winners' medal with them in 1934-35 as Hamilton Academical were beaten 2-1. Surprisingly though, that close season saw him transferred to Everton for a then Merseyside club record fee of £8,000.

During his time at Goodison Park, Gillick helped the Toffees win the Football League Championship in 1938-39, and appeared in five full internationals for Scotland. He had played for Everton against Rangers at Ibrox in the 1938 Empire Exhibition tournament, then guested for Rangers and his home-town team Airdrie during the hostilities.

He was brought back to Ibrox by Bill Struth in 1945, and that year another claim to fame was gained by him in Rangers' game against Moscow Dynamo. He stopped play to inform the referee that the Russian side had twelve players on the field!

Gillick developed into an outstanding forward who had excellent ball control and vision. In what was an exceptional post-war Rangers team, he formed a highly effective left-wing partnership with Willie Waddell. Gillick's delicate and instinctive passes would more often than not find the Rangers winger, who would overlap and use his lightning pace to terrorise opposition defences.

Gillick could score goals too, and in the club's League Championship-winning season of 1946-47, he netted 12 in 27 league games and a further five in eight League Cup ties, including one in the 4-0 League Cup Final victory over Aberdeen. With his short strides giving him a tremendous burst of speed and acceleration over 10 yards, Gillick was always a danger in and around the penalty area.

Despite moaning at everyone—referees, opponents and even his own team-mates—Gillick had a rather caustic sense of humour. When one of Rangers' opponents said to him 'We're on a £50 bonus', he replied: 'We're getting only a tenner, but then we always win our bonuses—you don't.' Also, when the Rangers manager instructed his players to be properly turned out and wear bowler hats, the story goes that Gillick used to carry his in a brown paper bag until he was within sight of Ibrox, when he would, still reluctantly, put it on his head!

Torry Gillick sadly died prematurely on 12 December 1971, the same day that perhaps the most famous of all Rangers players, Alan Morton, also died.

## ANDY GORAM

**Born:** Bury, 13 April 1964
**Rangers career:** 1991 to 1998
**Appearances and goals:**

| League | | FA Cup | | Lg Cup | | Europe | |
|---|---|---|---|---|---|---|---|
| **A** | **G** | **A** | **G** | **A** | **G** | **A** | **G** |
| 183/1 | 0 | 26 | 0 | 19 | 0 | 31 | 0 |

*Total appearances:* 259/1
*Total goals:* 0
**League Championships:** 1991-92; 1992-93; 1994-95; 1995-96; 1996-97
**Scottish Cup:** 1991-92; 1992-93; 1995-96
**League Cup:** 1992-93; 1996-97
**Honours:** 43 Scotland caps

Voted the greatest Rangers keeper of all time, Andy Goram in his career with the Light Blues gave dozens of genuinely world-class performances which epitomised his hatred of losing.

Goram started his career at Boundary Park, Oldham, not the sort of haunt which springs to mind as a hotbed of English soccer, but it was there that he learned his trade under Joe Royle. A Scotland debut, when the Tartan Army sang 'You're not English any more', was the fruit of his labours with the Latics. A £300,000 transfer to Hibs ensued as Goram set about his campaign to win a regular international place. That arrived, but there were still no honours at club level, and it was his hopes on that front, coupled with Walter Smith's needs for Scots for Rangers' European challenge, which saw him travel down the M8 from Edinburgh to Glasgow in June 1991 for a fee of £1 million.

Even then, things did not go especially smoothly, as Rangers' traditional up and down start to a season was even bumpier than normal and they

*Andy Goram keeps goal in a Rangers v Hearts match in 1992 (www.snspix.com)*

suffered some unlikely League defeats before a Goram error caused a League Cup semi-final loss to his former club Hibs. However, success was not long in coming, and in 1992-93 Rangers enjoyed a remarkable run of 44 games without defeat, lasting seven months in both Scottish and European competition. Crucial to the achievement of that season's treble were the heroics of Goram in goal, but it was his displays in Europe which really caught the eye, particularly away from home, where he was inspirational against Leeds and Marseille. Player and Footballer of the Year honours followed.

Injury caught up with him at the tail end of the 1993-94 season, and it was probably significant that Rangers' League-winning points tally at the end of the campaign was notably lower than in previous seasons, as Goram managed only eight matches. In the close season, Rangers boss Walter Smith placed Goram on the transfer list, having finally lost patience with the keeper's cavalier attitude towards training and his more thorough approach towards socialising!

However, Goram decided to stay and try to save his career, and his performances in 1994-95 as Rangers again won the League Championship were outstanding. It was around this time that it was reported in the press that Goram had a mild form of schizophrenia—fans responded with a chorus of 'Two Andy Gorams, there's only two Andy Gorams'!

Goram was in goal for the last of six of Rangers Nine-in-a-Row Championships. He was the rock which gave the Gers' defence the confidence to know that even when their lines had been breached, Goram would often pull off the impossible.

Andy Goram had superb anticipation, fast reflexes and immense courage. He had a great sense of positional play which made him quick to confront any danger. He was clever at closing down angles to reduce a striker's options and had amazing shot-stopping ability. Left one-on-one with an advancing striker, he would impose himself on his opponent by either standing up tall to beat off the shot, or advancing bravely to dive at his feet.

Known to team-mates simply as 'The Goalie', after his Rangers days Andy Goram had brief spells with Notts County and Sheffield United before joining Motherwell. He had appeared in 69 games for the Steelmen when a goalkeeping crisis at Old Trafford prompted Manchester United manager Sir Alex Ferguson to sign him as a stop-gap. He appeared in a couple of Premiership games before joining Coventry City. Following a knee injury that required keyhole surgery, Goram ended his career where he had started with Oldham, making his 'debut' in a 7-1 home defeat by Cardiff City!

A keen cricketer, having represented Scotland, Andy Goram is now a popular after-dinner speaker and regularly attends Rangers fans gatherings.

## RICHARD GOUGH

**Born:** Stockholm, Sweden, 5 April 1962
**Rangers career:** 1987 to 1997 and 1997 to 1998
**Appearances and goals:**

| League | | FA Cup | | Lg Cup | | Europe | |
|---|---|---|---|---|---|---|---|
| A | G | A | G | A | G | A | G |
| 318 | 25 | 37 | 2 | 37 | 3 | 36 | 4 |

*Total appearances:* 428
*Total goals:* 34
**League Championships:** 1988-89; 1989-90; 1990-91; 1991-92; 1992-93; 1993-94; 1994-95; 1995-96; 1996-97
**Scottish Cup:** 1991-92; 1992-93; 1995-96
**League Cup:** 1987-88; 1988-89; 1990-91; 1992-93; 1993-94; 1996-97
**Honours:** 61 Scotland caps

One of only three players to appear in Rangers' nine successive Championships during the 1980s and 1990s, Richard Gough was the one man who epitomised the effort, drive and skill which led the Light Blues to these successes.

Born to a Scottish father and Swedish mother, Richard Gough grew up in South Africa and began his career playing with the Wits University club. Looking to build a career in British football, Gough went on trial to Rangers but—somewhat ironically, in hindsight—was turned down. After that he was provisionally signed by Charlton Athletic, for whom his father Charlie had played. After returning to South Africa, he finally secured the move he wanted when he was signed by Scottish Premier Division team Dundee United in 1980.

He spent six seasons at Tannadice, helping United win the League Championship in 1982-83 and reach the finals of both the Scottish and League Cups in 1984-85. Voted Scottish PFA Player of the Year in 1986, he left United in August of that year, joining Tottenham Hotspur for a fee of £700,000. Immediately appointed captain by manager David Pleat, he led the North London club to the 1987 FA Cup Final and represented the Football League against the Rest of the World in the League's centenary match in August 1987. Unfortunately for Spurs, Gough's family were unable to settle in the south, and he was allowed to move to Rangers for a fee of £1.5 million.

Richard Gough was an accomplished player and an excellent timer of a tackle. He also had a fine touch, which made him a careful distributor of the ball once possession was won, and he was commanding in the air.

Gough made his League debut at right-back against Dundee United, and became an instant hit when, in his second game, he scored in the 2-2 draw with Celtic. Throughout the club's famous nine-in-a-row charge, Gough was a constant source of inspiration and leadership, especially after he replaced Terry Butcher as captain in 1990.

He was also a mainstay of the Scotland national team throughout the 1980s. Having made his debut against Switzerland in 1983, he went on to win 61 caps. One sad blemish on that record was the clash of wills between him and Scotland coach Andy Roxburgh in 1993, which was allowed to fester and then become outright war—robbing Gough of the chance to reach his century of caps.

Gough let it be known that he would be leaving Rangers at the end

*Richard Gough leaps high for the ball in the 1989 Skol Cup Final against Aberdeen (www.snspix.com)*

of the 1996-97 season, opting to play in the lower-grade Major League Soccer franchise of Kansas City Wizards. As the crescendo began to build in what was supposedly his last season at the club, Gough scored in the 2-0 home win over Celtic in September. The momentum was maintained with Gough's sixth League Cup Final victory, this time 4-3 over Hearts. But as the season reached its climax at Tannadice, Gough was missing through injury as Brian Laudrup scored the goal that gave Rangers Nine-in-a-Row. Gough was clearly overcome with emotion as he went on to the pitch to receive the trophy in what he believed would be his last act as a Rangers player.

But by October 1997 he was back at Ibrox, playing in 24 League games in what was his final season before spending another season in America with San Jose Clash. In March 1999 he joined Nottingham Forest, but was unable to prevent their relegation from the Premiership. He then joined Walter Smith's Everton, where he proved an inspirational figure both on and off the field.

After his second season on Merseyside was dogged by injuries, he had a brief spell in Australia before entering management with Livingston.

## JOHN GREIG

**Born:** Edinburgh, 11 September 1942
**Rangers career:** 1961 to 1978
**Appearances and goals:**

| League | | FA Cup | | Lg Cup | | Europe | |
|---|---|---|---|---|---|---|---|
| **A** | **G** | **A** | **G** | **A** | **G** | **A** | **G** |
| 494/4 | 87 | 72 | 9 | 121 | 17 | 64 | 7 |

*Total appearances:* 771/4
*Total goals:* 120
**League Championships:** 1962-63; 1963-64; 1974-75; 1975-76; 1977-78
**Scottish Cup:** 1962-63; 1963-64; 1965-66; 1972-73; 1975-76; 1977-78
**League Cup:** 1963-64; 1964-65; 1970-71; 1975-76; 1977-78
**European Cup Winners Cup:** 1971-72
**Honours:** 44 Scotland caps

There is little doubt that John Greig would be the name on anyone's short list for the greatest Rangers player of all time. The fans voted him the winner in a poll to find the Greatest Ever Ranger, and Greig received his award at a star-studded dinner in Glasgow in March 1999.

Edinburgh-born Greig was a Hearts supporter as a boy and was determined to play for the Tynecastle club. He only signed for Rangers because his father told him to when a scout visited the family home in Prestonfield. Greig made his Rangers debut in a League Cup match at Airdrie in September 1961 and scored in a 4-1 win for the Gers. Playing as

*John Greig celebrates after the 3-1 victory over Hearts in the 1976 Scottish Cup Final (www.snspix.com)*

a forward he scored seven goals in 11 games before impressing at wing-half on a summer tour to Russia.

Greig became a regular in the Rangers side in 1962-63, and after scoring a hat-trick in a 4-0 League Cup win over St Mirren, netted his first Old Firm goal on New Year's Day in a 4-0 defeat of Celtic. He ended that season with the first of his five League Championship medals and his first Scottish Cup winners' medal as Rangers beat Celtic in a final for the first time in 35 years with a 3-0 victory in a replay.

The following season brought the first of three Trebles, with Greig playing in every match of all three of the competitions. This was also the season that Greig won the first of his 44 full caps for Scotland, making his debut in a 1-0 win over England at Hampden Park in April 1964. Rangers won the League Cup again in 1964-65, beating Celtic 2-1 in the final, and the Scottish Cup the season after with a 1-0 victory over the Hoops in a replay. But the Treble-winning team was beginning to break up, and trophies were hard to come by as the rebuilding process began.

By now, John Greig was Rangers' captain, and under his forceful leadership, they reached the European Cup Winners' Cup Final in 1967, only to lose 1-0 to Bayern Munich after extra time. His captaincy style was inspirational, and he was skipper when Scotland took on then World Champions England at Wembley in 1967. Not only did he save a certain goal by heading off his own goal-line, but led his side to a memorable 3-2 win. In the dark days following the Ibrox tragedy when 66 people lost their lives in 1971, John Greig played the captain's role in leading the players as they attended the victims' funerals.

But by 1972, the glory returned as the Light Blues won the European Cup Winners Cup, beating Dynamo Moscow 3-2 in Barcelona. The following year he collected the Scottish Cup as Rangers beat Celtic 3-2, and in 1974-75 led Rangers to the League title after an absence of eleven years. The Rangers side now was the nucleus of the side that would win two Trebles in three years, and once again be the dominant force in Scottish football.

Rangers won the first of those two Trebles in 1975-76, with Greig receiving his fourth League Cup winners' medal as Celtic were beaten 1-0, and won the Scottish Cup for the fifth time as Hearts were defeated 3-1. The Treble was repeated in 1977-78 with Greig picking up his fifth League Cup winners' medal after Celtic had been beaten 2-1. A sixth Scottish Cup winners' medal came his way as Aberdeen were defeated by a similar scoreline. A few days after that Treble, Greig's life was to change dramatically.

Manager Jock Wallace quit his post and Greig was handed the job. His first season in charge was a rip-roaring success, with Rangers winning both domestic cup competitions and enjoying their best season in Europe since victory in 1971-72. The League was only lost in a titanic meeting with Celtic in the third-to-last game of the season! Rangers were to win another Scottish Cup and League Cup under Greig, but in October 1983, he resigned to be replaced by the returning Jock Wallace.

John Greig's heart, though, belonged to Rangers, and in 1990 he returned to Ibrox as the club's public relations officer. Made a director of the club in December 2003, Greig now works in the Youth Department at Murray Park, trying to unearth the next Rangers legend. He is also immortalised in a statue outside the ground, commemorating the tragic events of the Ibrox Stadium disaster of 1971.

## MARK HATELEY

**Born:** Liverpool, 7 November 1961
**Rangers career:** 1990 to 1995

**Appearances and goals:**

| League | | FA Cup | | Lg Cup | | Europe | |
|---|---|---|---|---|---|---|---|
| A | G | A | G | A | G | A | G |
| 162/7 | 88 | 17 | 10 | 18/1 | 11 | 17 | 6 |

*Total appearances:* 214/8
*Total goals:* 115
**League Championships:** 1990-91; 1991-92; 1992-93; 1993-94; 1994-95
**Scottish Cup:** 1991-92; 1992-93
**League Cup:** 1990-91; 1992-93; 1993-94
**Honours:** 32 England caps

---

Nicknamed 'Attila', Mark Hateley was undoubtedly one of the greatest strikers ever to wear the Light Blue of Rangers. Aggressive, powerful and sensational in the air, he formed a lethal strike partnership with Ally McCoist, yet after an unsteady start, he was at first hardly flavour of the month with the fans!

A big bustling centre-forward, Hateley first came to prominence at Coventry City, but it was at his next club Portsmouth that he won the first of his 32 England caps. In only his second appearance for the national side, Hateley scored against Brazil in the Maracana Stadium. He spent just one season at Fratton Park, scoring 25 goals in 44 games, including two hat-tricks in the space of four days. He joined AC Milan for £1 million, but after three years at the San Siro, he took the short hop to France and AS Monaco.

However, it was at Ibrox where Hateley produced his best and most consistent form, and was considered by many to be Graeme Souness's best signing for the club. By the time he and his team-mates reached the Wagnerian climax of the Englishman's first season for the club, Rangers had frittered away their lead. Aberdeen needed only a point for the title and Hateley had scored only three League goals since the turn of the year. Yet Hateley simply trampled on the Dons that day in May 1991, scoring twice in a display that gave the Gers the title. He netted a hat-trick on the opening day of the 1991-92 season as Rangers beat St Johnstone 6-0, and followed this with another later in the season against Airdrie. Not surprisingly, Rangers retained the title and won the Scottish Cup, with Hateley scoring one of the goals in the 2-1 final win over Airdrie.

Hateley's greatest season at Ibrox was 1992-93, when he provided countless highlights for the Rangers faithful. Without doubt the best remembered was his outstanding display in the Battle of Britain European Cup match against Leeds United. Denied inclusion in the England team by Graham Taylor, Hateley was regarded as a has-been in his own land, yet he destroyed the Yorkshire club, scoring with a magnificent 25-yard left-foot volley, and then setting up Ally McCoist's diving header with an inch-perfect cross.

He was the Division's top scorer in 1993-94, and was voted Player of the Year by the Scottish Football Writers Association, becoming the first Englishman to win this prestigious award. He left Rangers in 1995 to join former team-mate Ray Wilkins, who was then managing Queen's Park Rangers—it was thought family problems were the catalyst for the move.

However, in 1997, with Rangers trying to win their ninth title in a row and with a huge injury list, manager Walter Smith desperately needed a striker and re-signed Hateley for the vital game against Rangers' biggest rivals Celtic. Rangers won the game 1-0, but Hateley was sent off. However, most commentators thought that the mere presence of Hateley had given Rangers a psychological advantage and that it was a signing that had paid off. Rangers eventually won the League, with the game against Celtic seen as the unofficial clincher.

He managed Hull City, but left the Tigers after a couple of unproductive seasons which saw them struggling near the foot of the Football League and overshadowed by the constant fear of extinction.

Mark Hateley is now in the media business, commentating on Scottish Premier League matches for Setanta Sports and working in an ambassadorial role for Rangers.

## WILLIE HENDERSON

**Born:** Baillieston, 24 January 1944
**Rangers career:** 1960 to 1972
**Appearances and goals:**

| League | | FA Cup | | Lg Cup | | Europe | |
|---|---|---|---|---|---|---|---|
| **A** | **G** | **A** | **G** | **A** | **G** | **A** | **G** |
| 274/2 | 36 | 43/1 | 5 | 58/2 | 11 | 44/2 | 10 |

*Total appearances:* 419/7

*Total goals:* 62

**League Championships:** 1962-63; 1963-64
**Scottish Cup:** 1961-62; 1962-63; 1963-64; 1965-66
**League Cup:** 1963-64; 1970-71
**Honours:** 29 Scotland caps

Known as Wee Willie, which was hardly the most inventive nickname for the winger who stood just 5ft 4in, Henderson really was a Boy Wonder as he made his Rangers debut at 17, and a year later played for Scotland, netting on his debut against Wales—only Denis Law in the modern era played for the national side at a younger age.

His early displays hastened the departure of Alex Scott, and by the age of 19, Henderson had won every domestic honour the Scottish game could offer. Henderson also had bad eyesight and he wore contact lenses. People found this amusing, as they would often wonder how much better he might been had his eyesight been better. Legend has it that late on in an Old Firm

*Willie Henderson in action during the 1969-70 season (www.snspix.com)*

encounter he inquired on the sidelines 'How long to go, how long to go?' Jock Stein replied 'Go and ask the other dugout, you bloody fool—this is the Celtic bench!'

Those who saw him and, perhaps even more notably, played against him, have never encountered a quicker winger, but there was more to his game than lightning pace. Henderson's skill at beating defenders was great to watch, his crossing was invariably accurate and he scored a number of important goals too —particularly against Slavia Sofia in the European Cup Winners' Cup semi-final of 1967.

He was part of the famous early 1960s side which many regard as the finest Rangers have ever had. A clean sweep of honours in 1963-64 was indicative of that. During his time with Rangers he won the Scottish League twice, the Scottish Cup four times and the League Cup twice. He was also part of the Rangers team that got to finals of the 1960-61 and 1966-67 European Cup Winners' Cup competitions, and was part of the Rangers campaign that eventually brought home the trophy in the 1971-72 season.

However, there was a sad end to his Rangers career, as Henderson missed out on becoming a European winner when he left the club under something of a cloud before the final in Barcelona. He had played a leading role in helping Rangers on their travels, most notably with an extra-time goal in the quarter-final against Sporting Lisbon. However, he had a fall-out with manager Willie Waddell and was sitting on a beach in South Africa as his former team-mates wrote their names into the club's history by beating Dynamo Moscow 3-2 He later admitted that missing the game was one of the worst moments of his career.

He signed for Sheffield Wednesday, becoming a great favourite with the Hillsborough faithful in his two seasons with the club. His last appearance for the Owls was on the final day of the 1973-74 season against Bolton Wanderers. It was a match Wednesday had to win to avoid relegation to the Third Division. They won the game 1-0. Henderson later played for Hong Kong Rangers before returning to Scotland to appear in a handful of games for Airdrie.

Willie Henderson currently runs a hotel in Lanarkshire. On match days he works for Rangers in their Hospitality Department, and he invariably lights up proceedings with his many stories and quips.


## JOHNNY HUBBARD

**Born:** Pretoria, South Africa, 16 December 1930
**Rangers career:** 1949 to 1959
**Appearances and goals:**

| League | | FA Cup | | Lg Cup | | Europe | |
|---|---|---|---|---|---|---|---|
| **A** | **G** | **A** | **G** | **A** | **G** | **A** | **G** |
| 172 | 77 | 19 | 5 | 41 | 23 | 6 | 1 |

*Total appearances:* 238
*Total goals:* 106
**League Championships:** 1952-53; 1955-56; 1956-57
**Scottish Cup:** 1952-53
**Honours:** 1 South Africa cap

Johnny Hubbard arrived at Ibrox from South Africa in the summer of 1949. He had been recommended to the Light Blues by the former Hibernian player Alex Prior, who was at that time a photographer in South Africa and who had described Hubbard as 'the best player in the Union'.

Standing just 5ft 4ins, Hubbard was a fragile-looking figure and certainly did not impress Rangers manager Bill Struth on their first meeting, but when the Gers' boss saw his skill on the ball he signed him immediately.

A tricky, dribbling left-winger and a master of the penalty-kick, Hubbard rapidly became a great favourite with the Rangers fans and was to remain at the club for a decade.

Hubbard converted a phenomenal 54 out of 57 penalties during his time with the club, including 23 successive scores until he missed one against Dave Walker in January 1956 in the match against Airdrie. He did score in the match though, as Rangers won 4-0 with Sammy Baird grabbing a hat-trick. The two other keepers who achieved a modest immortality by stopping a Johnny Hubbard penalty were Jimmy Brown of Kilmarnock and Bert Slater of Falkirk.

Although Rangers didn't lose a home game in the League in 1954-55, they weren't as successful away from Ibrox and finished third behind champions Aberdeen and Celtic. Rangers did however beat the Hoops in the Ne'er Day fixture 4-1, with Hubbard netting his first hat-trick for the club. In fact, his three goals all came in the last 18 minutes of the game.

He helped Rangers win successive League Championships in 1955-56 and 1956-57, and in the former of those seasons, netted 10 goals in nine League Cup games, along with a goal every other game in the League. His total of 27 in all competitions was his best during his stay at Ibrox. In 1956-57 Hubbard provided most of the ammunition which brought Billy Simpson and Max Murray 50 goals between them.

Though Rangers didn't complete a hat-trick of Championship victories in 1957-58, Johnny Hubbard had his best season in terms of League goals. His total of 18 in just 24 games included all four in a 4-0 win at Falkirk. He also netted three goals in the club's run to the League Cup Final, but his side was well beaten 7-1 on the day.

In 1958-59, Hubbard's last season with the club, he netted 10 goals in his eight starts, including hat-tricks against Airdrie—though Rangers lost 5-4—and Dunfermline Athletic, who were thrashed 7-1, the trebles coming in successive away games. In April 1959, the South African international, whose only appearance for his country was against Scotland, was transferred to Bury for a fee of £6,000.

He spent three seasons at Gigg Lane, helping the Shakers win the Third Division Championship in 1960-61. On hanging up his boots, he returned to Scotland and became a recreation officer in the Prestwick area of Ayrshire.

## PIETER HUISTRA

**Born:** Goenga, Holland, 18 January 1967
**Rangers career:** 1990 to 1995
**Appearances and goals:**

| League | | FA Cup | | Lg Cup | | Europe | |
|---|---|---|---|---|---|---|---|
| **A** | **G** | **A** | **G** | **A** | **G** | **A** | **G** |
| 87/38 | 22 | 5/5 | I | 12/3 | I | 8/I | 2 |

*Total appearances:* 112/47
*Total goals:* 26
**League Championships:** 1990-91; 1991-92; 1992-93; 1993-94; 1994-95
**Scottish Cup:** 1992-93
**League Cup:** 1990-91; 1993-94
**Honours:** 8 Holland caps

Pieter Huistra was erratic, certainly, but on his day he was a real asset. His arrival from Twente Enschede was fairly low-key by Rangers standards, but he demonstrated during the 1990-91 season that there was no reason to question his ability. He scored four times and set up countless other goals, as he more than justified his £300,000 fee.

He was one of a succession of wingers invested in by the Ibrox club during the 1980s and 1990s—Cooper, Walters, Gordon, Huistra, Laudrup, even Mikhailitchenko at times—and the return was hours of fun for the fans as opposition defenders were tormented.

The one doubt, which persisted throughout his stay, was his durability, and this was to cost him a couple of Cup Final appearances as Walter Smith opted for a more physical approach. All's well that ends well, though, and Piet left Scotland with a full set of domestic medals after appearing in the League Cup wins of 1990-91 and 1993-94 and the Scottish Cup triumph of 1992-93.

However, it was in Europe that he probably enjoyed his finest moment in the Light Blue of Rangers, with a vital strike in the Champions League run of 1992-93 against Bruges. Trailing by a goal to the Belgians, Huistra took the opportunity to put one over on his close friends and neighbours with a superb equaliser, to make sure the momentum that nearly carried the Gers to the Champions Cup Final was maintained.

Towards the tail end of the 1993-94 season, it became apparent that he would be surplus to requirements, as Walter Smith sought to add Scots to the squad. He went for trials with Queen's Park Rangers and German club Duisburg, but both came to nothing. It was probably a relief for the Dutchman, as with Rangers eliminated from Europe, he came back into the League side for his longest run of starts since joining the club and played superbly. It was during this period that his £500,000 transfer to Sanfrecce Hiroshima in the J League was arranged, a mutually beneficial move which allowed Rangers to make a profit on the player and Huistra to make himself financially secure for the rest of his life.

A skilful winger, he may not have been a great but he was a player who put more into the club than he took out, and one who developed a great affinity for its traditions. If ever there was a perfect swansong to a Rangers career it came in January 1995 at Brockville. He capped his last game for the club with two goals which helped seal a 3-2 victory over Falkirk. He left to the chants of 'There's only one Pieter Huistra', to provide him with some happy memories of his time at Ibrox.

## COLIN JACKSON

**Born:** London, 8 October 1946
**Rangers career:** 1963 to 1982
**Appearances and goals:**

| League | | FA Cup | | Lg Cup | | Europe | |
|---|---|---|---|---|---|---|---|
| **A** | **G** | **A** | **G** | **A** | **G** | **A** | **G** |
| 339/2 | 23 | 53 | 8 | 74/1 | 8 | 37 | 1 |

*Total appearances:* 503/3
*Total goals:* 40
**League Championships:** 1974-75; 1975-76; 1977-78
**Scottish Cup:** 1975-76; 1977-78; 1978-79
**League Cup:** 1970-71; 1975-76; 1977-78; 1978-79; 1981-82
**Honours:** 8 Scotland caps

Colin Jackson was a commanding centre-half who gave Rangers 20 years' monumental service. Tall and slender, he excelled at reading games and denying the opposition goalscoring opportunities. Jackson's aerial ability was second to none but there were times during his Ibrox career that he had to be extremely patient, often spending weeks on end in the club's reserve side behind the likes of Derek Johnstone and Ronnie McKinnon.

Rangers had signed the London-born Jackson from Sunnybank Athletic in Aberdeen, from under the noses of the Pittodrie scouting staff. One of only a handful of Rangers players born outside Scotland to be capped for the national team, he was never on the losing side in any of his eight full international appearances, and managed to get on the scoresheet in the 2-2 draw against Wales at Ninian Park in May 1975.

Having played an important role in the majority of the club's matches during their 1971-72 European Cup Winners' Cup campaign, Colin Jackson's greatest disappointment came when he failed a late fitness test on the eve of the final against Moscow Dynamo in Barcelona, a match Rangers won 3-2, with two goals from Willie Johnston and a third by Colin Stein.

In complete contrast, probably the greatest highlight of his long and illustrious career came in the dying moments of the 1978-79 League Cup Final against Aberdeen, when, with the referee poised to blow for full-time, he headed home the winning goal from a corner-kick.

Colin Jackson went on to win three League Championships and was on the winning side in three Scottish Cup Finals and four League Cup Finals—with an 11-year gap between his first success against Celtic in 1970-71 and Dundee United in 1981-82.

One of the Scottish League's most effective central defenders, he had scored 40 goals in 506 competitive games for the Light Blues when, in September 1982, he left to play for Morton.

He left Cappielow Park a year later to join Partick Thistle, but again after just one season, he parted company with the Jags to become a partner in an East Kilbride printing firm.

## SANDY JARDINE

**Born:** Edinburgh, 31 December 1948
**Rangers career:** 1964 to 1982
**Appearances and goals:**

| League | | FA Cup | | Lg Cup | | Europe | |
|---|---|---|---|---|---|---|---|
| **A** | **G** | **A** | **G** | **A** | **G** | **A** | **G** |
| 431/20 | 42 | 60/4 | 8 | 106/1 | 25 | 50/2 | 2 |

*Total appearances: 647/27*
*Total goals: 77*
**League Championships:** 1974-75; 1975-76; 1977-78;
**Scottish Cup:** 1972-73; 1975-76; 1977-78; 1978-79; 1980-81
**League Cup:** 1970-71; 1975-76; 1977-78; 1978-79; 1981-82
**European Cup Winners Cup:** 1971-72
**Honours:** 38 Scotland caps

Sandy Jardine was a world-class full-back. Twice voted Player of the Year in Scotland and an important member of the Treble teams of 1975-76 and 1977-78 as well as the European Cup Winners' Cup success, only John Greig has made more post-war appearances for the club.

Jardine had played in a variety of positions—wing-half, inside-forward and even centre-forward—before Rangers boss Willie Waddell switched him to full-back, where he proved as cultured, elegant footballer. He had made his Rangers debut at right-half against Hearts in February 1967, just a week after the Gers had suffered the shock of losing 1-0 to Berwick Rangers in the Scottish Cup. Hearts were beaten 5-1, and Jardine kept his place in the side for the rest of the season and played in the European Cup Winners' Cup Final against Bayern Munich in May 1967, a match Rangers lost 1-0.

At the beginning of the 1968-69 season, Jardine found himself wearing the No. 9 shirt. He played in 12 consecutive games, netting 11 goals including four in a 7-1 defeat of Queen's Park in the Glasgow Cup. That and the following season saw the Rangers team switched around as a successful formula was sought. Then for the last three games of the 1969-70 season, manager Waddell moved him to full-back. A player with attacking instincts as well as being a strong tackler, he soon demonstrated that he had the speed and skill to become a master of the role.

Jardine won his first major trophy in 1970 after Rangers defeated Celtic

*Sandy Jardine playing against Dundee United in 1979 (www.snspix.com)*

1-0 in the League Cup Final, and made the first of 39 appearances for Scotland off the bench against Denmark at Hampden Park. His first international start came in October 1971 against Portugal, when he marked the great Eusebio out of the game as Scotland won 2-1. He went on to play in the World Cup Finals in Germany in 1974 and Argentina in 1978. Jardine and Celtic's Danny McGrain formed a first-class partnership as the

Scotland full-back pairing on 19 occasions, and were spoken of as the best in the 1974 tournament.

He played in every round of the 1971-72 European Cup Winners' Cup as Rangers achieved glory by winning the trophy 3-2 against Dynamo Moscow in Barcelona. In fact, it was Jardine's crucial goal in the semi-final second leg against Bayern Munich that had put the Gers ahead and on their way to the Final.

It was towards the end of that successful European campaign that Jardine embarked on a sequence of 171 consecutive appearances, speaking volumes for both his ability and his fitness.

In 1974-75, Rangers won the League Championship for the first time in 11 years, with Sandy Jardine again ever present. However, there was better to come with two Trebles in the space of three years. The trophies included two League Cup Final victories over Celtic and Scottish Cup Final wins, 3-1 over Hearts and 2-1 overAberdeen. During the 1974-75 League Cup run, Jardine netted a hat-trick against Airdrie.

He added to his collection of domestic honours in 1978-79 as Rangers retained both the League and Scottish Cups. It was at the start of the following season that Sandy Jardine scored the goal of his career. Winning possession on the edge of his own penalty area in the Dryborough Cup Final against Celtic, he ran almost the length of the field, beating defender after defender, before cutting inside the Celtic box and unleashing a powerful left-foot shot that almost burst the net!

He was to win two more Cup winners' medals—a 4-1 victory over Dundee United in a replayed Scottish Cup Final in 1981, and later that year a 2-1 League Cup Final success over the same opposition. After playing in every League game in 1981-82, Jardine was released and joined Hearts. With Jardine as their sweeper, the Jam Tarts came close to honours in 1985-86, finishing as runners-up in both the Championship and Scottish Cup.

He later became player/assistant-manager at Tynecastle, and then joint manager until 1988. After working as a marketing manager for the Scottish Breweries, he is now back at Ibrox as the club's Sales and Marketing Manager.

## KAI JOHANSEN

**Born:** Odense, Denmark, 23 February 1940
**Died:** 12 May 2007
**Rangers career:** 1965 to 1970
**Appearances and goals:**

| League | | FA Cup | | Lg Cup | | Europe | |
|---|---|---|---|---|---|---|---|
| A | G | A | G | A | G | A | G |
| 158 | 4 | 22 | 3 | 32 | 2 | 27 | 1 |

*Total appearances:* 239
*Total goals:* 10
**Scottish Cup:** 1965-66
**Honours:** 20 Denmark caps

A Danish international full-back, Kai Johansen was a player of outstanding talent, joining Rangers from Morton for a fee of £20,000 in the summer of 1965. Seen as a replacement for Bobby Shearer, this was at a time when the Morton impresario Hal Stewart was importing Scandinavian players galore.

A player who was able to play in either full-back berth, he took a little time to adjust to life at Ibrox, mainly because of the restrictions imposed on his play by Rangers' boss Scot Symon. He believed that defenders, and in particular full-backs, should never cross the halfway line!

Unfortunately for Symon, Johansen was a modern attacking full-back, highly rated throughout the whole of Europe. He had a crouching style, always attacking the ball and coming forward at great speed.

He didn't score many goals during his stay with Rangers, but the first he did score saw him enter Rangers folklore. The Scottish Cup Final of 1966 between Rangers and arch-rivals Celtic ended goalless, with Johansen having a difficult time against Celtic's John Hughes. The final was replayed the following Wednesday, and though the game was something of an anti-climax, it was settled ten minutes from time. Winger Willie Johnston beat three Hoops defenders and crossed low into the centre, where he found Willie Henderson. The right-winger's shot was cleared by Bobby Murdoch, but only straight to Kai Johansen, who from fully 25 yards out unleashed a cracking low drive for what proved to be the only goal of the game.

In the 1967-68 League Cup competition, Rangers were unbeaten when they faced Celtic at Parkhead, having drawn against the Hoops in an earlier meeting. Willie Henderson had put Rangers ahead as early as the 7th minute, and Bobby Lennox had a 'goal' wiped out on the stroke of half-time. Rangers defended grimly, but in a breakaway attack, Willie Johnston smashed a shot against the Celtic crossbar. With a little over ten minutes remaining, Celtic's John Clark fouled Henderson and the referee awarded a penalty.

Johansen's spot-kick struck the underside of the bar and, as the ball bounced out, the Dane illegally hit it home, completely oblivious to the presence of the waiting and expectant Andy Penman!

One of the game's most prodigious talkers, Kai Johansen was extremely popular among Rangers supporters of the day. On hanging up his boots in 1970, he ran a pub in Glasgow city centre before later running a bar on Spain's Costa del Sol. On his return to his native Denmark, he became a players' agent and later operated for a spell in South Africa.

# MO JOHNSTON

**Born:** Glasgow, 13 April 1963
**Rangers career:** 1989 to 1991
**Appearances and goals:**

| League | | FA Cup | | Lg Cup | | Europe | |
|---|---|---|---|---|---|---|---|
| A | G | A | G | A | G | A | G |
| 75/1 | 31 | 4/1 | 1 | 13 | 9 | 6 | 5 |

*Total appearances:* 98/2
*Total goals:* 46
**League Championships:** 1989-90; 1990-91
**Honours:** 38 Scotland caps

---

Maurice 'Mo' Johnston, an ex-Celtic, Scottish international forward, had agreed to rejoin the Hoops from French club Nantes in the summer of 1989. Indeed, he had been paraded in front of the Celtic supporters prior to the Cup Final. But at the last moment, Rangers' boss Graeme Souness stepped in and secured the striker's signature in a £1.5 million deal.

Johnston started out with junior side Milton Battlefield before being snapped up by Scottish First Division Partick Thistle in July 1980. In just over three years with the Jags, he scored 41 goals from 85 games before signing for Watford. He proved to be an inspired signing by the Hornets, following the departure of their leading marksman Luther Blissett to AC Milan.

He netted a hat-trick against Wolves in only eight minutes in what was his third outing for Watford .At the end of his first season he had scored 20 goals in 29 games and helped the club reach the FA Cup Final for the first time in their history. He had already had the satisfaction of winning the first of his 38 caps for Scotland against Wales in February 1984.

Johnston had his wishes granted during the early stages of the 1984-85 season when allowed to return home with Celtic. He scored 52 goals in 99 games and won League Championship and Scottish Cup winners' medals in three years at Parkhead before signing for French club Nantes.

After initially claiming he would never return to Scotland, Johnston reconsidered and appeared at a press conference to announce that he would rejoin Celtic at the end of his contract with the French club. However, after a change of mind, he signed for Rangers. This unprecedented move managed to anger some supporters of both Celtic and Rangers. There were some Rangers fans who saw the signing of a Roman Catholic—who was also a high profile player and supporter of their most bitter rivals—as a betrayal of the club's traditions. Other supporters viewed the signing enthusiastically, the one-upmanship of securing the coveted Johnston outweighing whatever other reservations might have existed on the grounds of religion or footballing enmity.

Johnston was not the first Roman Catholic to sign for Rangers, but his signing was by far the highest profile one during a period in which Rangers very publicly committed the club to a signing policy which took no account of religion.

A proven goalscorer at all his previous clubs, his pace and reflexes taking him into the striking places, he formed an effective strike partnership with Ally McCoist and was the club's top scorer in 1989-90 with 15 goals in 36 league games, helping the Gers win the League Championship. The following season, as well as helping Rangers retain their title, he netted a hat-trick (five goals over the two legs) as Rangers beat Valletta FC 10-0 on aggregate. He started the 1991-92 season, his last with the club and one in which the club won a fourth successive Championship, by scoring four goals in the 6-0 League Cup romp over Queen's Park. He had scored 46 goals in 100 games in all competitions when he moved to Everton.

It seemed like a shrewd move to boost the Merseyside club's flagging fortunes, but he was unable to provide any real spark and returned home to play for Hearts and later Falkirk, before crossing the Atlantic to Major League soccer for Kansas City Wizards. Part of the team that won the MLS Cup in 2000, he later hung up his boots and worked as head coach for the Metro Stars. He is now head coach for the newly formed Major League Soccer club Toronto FC.

## WILLIE JOHNSTON

**Born:** Glasgow, 19 December 1946
**Rangers career:** 1964 to 1973 and 1980 to 1982
**Appearances and goals:**

| League | | FA Cup | | Lg Cup | | Europe | |
|---|---|---|---|---|---|---|---|
| A | G | A | G | A | G | A | G |
| 236/10 | 91 | 42 | 10 | 60/5 | 16 | 40 | 8 |

*Total appearances:* 378/15
*Total goals:* 125
**Scottish Cup:** 1965-66; 1980-81
**League Cup:** 1964-65; 1970-71
**European Cup Winners Cup:** 1971-72
**Honours:** 22 Scotland caps

Controversy was certainly never far away from Willie Johnston, a dazzling winger with electrifying pace, terrific skill and a great strike rate. Yet, he may be better remembered for an appalling disciplinary record which saw him sent off over 10 times and for being banned from the international game following a drugs test at the 1978 World Cup Finals in Argentina.

'Bud', as he was known, signed for Rangers from Lochore Welfare in Fife in 1964, and made his debut against St Johnstone in August of that year. A

*Willie Johnston in action for Rangers in 1970 (www.snspix.com)*

couple of months later, he was a member of the Light Blues side that beat Celtic 2-1 to lift the League Cup. So skilled was the winger that in the space of six months he rose from Scottish youth international to full international, making his senior debut in a World Cup qualifying match against Poland.

Initially he played at inside-left, forming a devastating wing partnership with the experienced Davie Wilson. A great entertainer, Johnston had a great rapport with the Rangers fans. But he could also be argumentative, especially with match officials! Having finished the 1968-69 season as the club's top scorer with 18 goals in 29 games and netted a hat-trick against Dunfermline Athletic in the club's successful League Cup campaign of 1970-71, his contribution to Rangers' finest hour on foreign soil the following season was vital. It was Johnston's goals either side of half-time in the game against Moscow Dynamo that clinched the European Cup Winners' Cup.

The first part of Johnston's Ibrox career earned him a Scottish Cup and two League Cup medals to go with his European gong. His great pace and amazing dribbling skills had terrorised Scottish League defences and earned him a move to First Division West Bromwich Albion in December 1972.

Johnston played well at the Hawthorns, although he was sent off against Brighton for kicking the referee up the backside! His displays brought him into the squad of Scotland players for the World Cup Finals in Argentina. Following the match against Peru, which Scotland lost 3-1, he was routinely tested and found to have taken a banned substance. He was withdrawn from the tournament, sent home and banned from playing for Scotland ever again.

Although Johnston's arrival at West Bromwich was too late to prevent the club's relegation in 1973, he was a vital part of Johnny Giles' promotion-winning side three years later, and went on to see Albion established as a top flight side before leaving to play for Vancouver Whitecaps in March 1979. After a loan spell with Birmingham City, Johnston returned to Ibrox for a couple more seasons under John Greig.

In his second spell with the club, he helped Rangers win the Scottish Cup, bearing Dundee United 4-1, but earlier in the campaign he had been sent off in a League Cup tie against Aberdeen. The winger later had brief spells playing with Hearts and Falkirk, before he, having earned a special place in the Ibrox Hall of Fame after scoring 125 goals in 393 games, retired from the game and became a licensee in Kirkcaldy.

## DEREK JOHNSTONE

**Born:** Dundee, 4 November 1953
**Rangers career:** 1970 to 1983 and 1985 to 1986
**Appearances and goals:**

| League | | FA Cup | | Lg Cup | | Europe | |
|---|---|---|---|---|---|---|---|
| **A** | **G** | **A** | **G** | **A** | **G** | **A** | **G** |
| 357/12 | 132 | 55/2 | 30 | 82/3 | 39 | 31/4 | 9 |

*Total appearances:* 525/21
*Total goals:* 210
**League Championships:** 1974-75; 1975-76; 1977-78
**Scottish Cup:** 1972-73; 1975-76; 1977-78; 1978-79; 1980-81
**League Cup:** 1970-71; 1975-76; 1977-78; 1978-79; 1981-82
**European Cup Winners Cup:** 1971-72
**Honours:** 14 Scotland caps

Derek Johnstone was an outstanding Rangers player, who was so versatile he could play at centre-half, centre-forward or in midfield, and did so for both club and country. He was just 16 years and 355 days old when he scored the winner in the 1970-71 League Cup Final, and two years later was a member of the Rangers side that triumphed in Europe.

A boyhood Dundee United supporter, he scored twice on his Rangers debut as Cowdenbeath were beaten 5-0, and prior to the League Cup Final, his only other appearance had been as a substitute against Motherwell. On the eve of the big game, Rangers manager Willie Waddell told him to get a good night's sleep, but the excitement was too much and he tossed and turned all night. It made little difference to the youngster the next day: he rose to meet a cross, timing his header perfectly, and it flashed into the Celtic net for the only goal of the game. Not only was it the Gers' first trophy for four years, it ended a run of League Cup successes by the Hoops.

Johnstone was devastating with his head but was also surprisingly quick on the ground. In the club's European Cup Winners' Cup success of 1971-72, Johnstone played up front in the quarter and semi-finals but reverted to centre-half for the 3-2 final defeat of Moscow Dynamo. Over the next couple of seasons, Johnstone continued playing at centre-half and in 1972-73 helped Rangers win the Scottish Cup with a 3-2 defeat of Celtic.

But in 1974-75, when the Ibrox club won the League Championship for the first time in 11 years, he divided his time between attack and defence, scoring 14 goals in 27 games. Not surprisingly, he was Rangers' leading marksman when they won the trebles in seasons 1975-76 and 1977-78. Celtic

*Derek Johnstone (centre), Tommy McLean (right) and Colin Stein (left) celebrate after winning the 1972 European Cup Winners' Cup in Barcelona (www.snspix.com)*

were beaten 1-0 in the League Cup Final, and the Championship was won with a 1-0 victory at Dundee United with Johnstone scoring the game's only goal after 22 seconds. A week later, in the Scottish Cup Final, Johnstone actually scored before the official kick-off time! His goal was timed at 45 seconds, but the referee had begun the game early and Johnstone had the ball in the net before the scheduled 3pm start. He went on to score twice as Hearts were beaten 3-1.

His total of 25 goals in 33 games in the 1977-78 season—his highest for the club—included hat-tricks in the 4-1 win over Motherwell and the 5-0 rout of Ayr United. Celtic were again beaten in the League Cup Final 2-1, and in the Scottish Cup Final, Johnstone netted the winner as Aberdeen also went down 2-1.

Johnstone won 14 caps for Scotland and was a member of the national squad for the 1978 World Cup Finals in Argentina but was not selected to play in any of the matches, an omission that rankled with Rangers fans, especially as he had scored in two of the three preceding international matches!

Back on the domestic front, the Light Blues retained the League Cup in 1978-79, but in the Scottish Cup final they needed two replays to overcome Hibernian, with Johnstone scoring twice from midfield as Rangers eventually won 3-2. In 1980-81 Rangers again reached the Scottish Cup Final, but Johnstone was left out of the side that played out a goalless draw with Dundee United. He was back in the side for the replay, and though he didn't score, he helped his side to a 4-1 win.

Derek Johnstone had played in two Treble-winning sides, had won three League Championship medals, five Scottish Cups, five League Cups and a European Cup Winners Cup—he had also been Rangers club captain for three years.

In 1983 he was transferred to Chelsea, but failed to hold down a regular place and in January 1985, was back at Ibrox for a second spell. Though this was not a success, he was coming to the end of his playing days and he left to spend a brief spell as manager of Partick Thistle. Since then, he has worked extensively in the football media, including for BBC Scotland, Radio Clyde and the Glasgow *Evening Times*.

## STEFAN KLOS

**Born:** Dortmund, Germany, 19 August 1971
**Rangers career:** 1997 to present
**Appearances and goals:**

| League | | FA Cup | | Lg Cup | | Europe | |
|---|---|---|---|---|---|---|---|
| **A** | **G** | **A** | **G** | **A** | **G** | **A** | **G** |
| 208 | 0 | 29 | 0 | 14 | 0 | 47 | 0 |

*Total appearances:* 298
*Total goals:* 0
**League Championships:** 1988-99; 1999-2000; 2002-03; 2004-05
**Scottish Cup:** 1998-99; 1999-2000; 2001-02; 2002-03
**League Cup:** 2001-02; 2002-03

Signed from Borussia Dortmund on Christmas Eve 1997 for a fee of £700,000, following a protracted contract dispute, goalkeeper Stefan Klos proved a great Christmas present! He had a hard act to follow in Andy Goram, but since putting pen to paper, he has more than proved his worth. So much so that he has earned the nickname of 'Der Goalie'.

Before arriving at Ibrox, Klos had spent over ten years with Borussia Dortmund, surprisingly never winning full international honours but gaining plenty of European experience and winning the Bundesliga. One of the highlights of his spell in his native Germany was being between the posts when his side won the Champions Cup, after beating Juventus 3-1 in May 1997.

Since keeping a clean sheet on his debut on Boxing Day 1997, as Rangers beat St Johnstone 1-0, Klos has been one of the club's most consistent performers. In his first season with the club, he helped Rangers win the League Championship and defeat Celtic 1-0 in the Scottish Cup Final.

Rangers retained both trophies the following season, finishing 21 points ahead of runners-up Celtic and beating Aberdeen 4-0 to keep a firm hold of the Scottish Cup.

During the following season, Chairman David Murray hailed the 'tremendous courage' of Stefan Klos after it emerged the Rangers goalkeeper had risked a lifetime with arthritis to assist the club's Champions League quest. Klos was warned to stop playing and seek urgent medical attention for ankle ligaments which split and became infected. He kept a clean sheet in a goalless draw with Galatasaray before flying out for specialist treatment at a Munich clinic.

Rangers won both domestic cup competitions in 2001-02 before winning the treble the following season. Klos, who was ever-present, capped a fine campaign by collecting the Carling Player of the Year and the Player's Player of the Year awards. One of the few players who could hold his head up high the following season, his experience was vital to Rangers and the development of their young goalkeepers.

Prior to the start of the 2004-05 season, Stefan Klos, who was rated extremely highly by Alex McLeish, was automatic choice for club captain after Craig Moore was transfer-listed. The campaign saw him start well, keeping 17 clean sheets in 34 games. However, a torn cruciate ligament in his knee, suffered during training in January, meant the German had to sit the rest of the season out.

His replacement Ronald Waterreus kept his place for the start of the 2005-06 season, this in spite of Klos regaining full fitness. He looked set to challenge new signing Lionel Letizi for the No.1 slot after Paul le Guen's arrival at the start of the 2006-07 season, but he suffered a biking injury which gave long-term third choice Allan McGregor the chance to impress. In October 2006 Klos returned to fitness, and after a number of reserve appearances, played his first game against Hapoel Tel-Aviv in the UEFA Cup after McGregor was sent off! At the end of the 2006-07 season, Klos left Ibrox. At the time of his departure, he was Rangers longest-serving player.

## BRIAN LAUDRUP

**Born:** Vienna, Austria, 22 February 1969
**Rangers career:** 1994 to 1998
**Appearances and goals:**

| League | | FA Cup | | Lg Cup | | Europe | |
|---|---|---|---|---|---|---|---|
| A | G | A | G | A | G | A | G |
| 114/2 | 34 | 13 | 5 | 4 | 3 | 16/1 | 3 |

*Total appearances:* 147/3
*Total goals:* 45
**League Championships:** 1994-95; 1995-96; 1996-97

**Scottish Cup:** 1995-96
**League Cup:** 1996-97
**Honours:** 82 Denmark caps

Many Rangers fans consider Danish international Brian Laudrup the greatest talent to have played for the Ibrox club. A true genius with a football, Laudrup was the complete master, terrifying opposition defences any time he was near the ball.

Though Danish, Laudrup was born in Vienna. He grew up in a footballing family; his father Finn was a Danish international and his elder brother Michael was also a world-class player, playing with, among others, Juventus, Barcelona and Real Madrid.

Brian Laudrup started his career with Brondby before a move to Bayer Uerdingen in Germany followed, but after just one season, he moved on to Bayern Munich. One of the biggest club sides in Germany should have been the ideal place for Laudrup to showcase his talents, but injuries persistently interrupted his progress and it was in a Danish shirt that he began to realise the potential which had always been in him.

The Danes were brought in to make up the numbers in the European Championship Finals in Sweden in 1992 after Yugoslavia dissolved into civil war, but shocked the world by going all the way to the final and then beating favourites Germany 2-0. Laudrup was outstanding and captured the imagination of scouts throughout Europe, including those of Fiorentina who were to be his next club. Florence was not a happy hunting ground, and as his team struggled he went out on loan to AC Milan.

Come the summer of 1994 and Laudrup was looking for a new club, yet he had acquired a reputation of never staying anywhere very long. Rangers stepped in and bought the Dane

*Brian Laudrup in action for Rangers*
*(www.snspix.com)*

for a fee of £2.3 million—as it turned out it was a snip! From his first game against Motherwell, Laudrup was a revelation, supplying an inch-perfect cross for Hateley to head home and then running diagonally through midfield before releasing a pass for Duncan Ferguson to net the second. Though he wore the No.11 shirt, Laudrup was given a free role by Rangers' boss Walter Smith, and scored 10 goals in 33 games as Rangers won their seventh consecutive League Championship. Not surprisingly he was named Player of the Year by both the Football Writers and the Footballers' Association.

Joined in midfield by Paul Gascoigne for the 1995-96 season, Laudrup helped Rangers win their eight successive title but it was in the Scottish Cup that he scored the goal of the season. It came in the semi-final against Celtic. The scores were level at 1-1 when he collected the ball in midfield and played a one-two with Gordon Durie. But the return ball came from behind him, and while running, the Dane brought it under control with his chest before chipping it over the keeper for the winner.

The Cup Final against Hearts saw Laudrup give a virtuoso performance as Hearts were beaten 5-1, with Durie netting a hat-trick. However, it was the Dane who grabbed the headlines, making all of Durie's goals and scoring the other two himself.

As Rangers completed their nine-in-a-row in 1996-97, Laudrup was the club's top scorer with 17 goals in 33 games. These included a fine individual goal against Aberdeen, and the only goal of the game against Celtic with a powerfully struck 25-yard drive. He also headed home the goal against Dundee United at Tannadice to clinch the League Championship. Once again it was Laudrup who was the Football Writers' Player of the Year.

The 1997-98 season was something of an anti-climax, and after playing for Denmark in the 1998 World Cup Finals, he opted for a move to Chelsea. One of the most talented entertainers in Rangers' history, he later had a brief spell with FC Copenhagen before ending his career with Ajax.

## JOHN LITTLE

**Born:** Calgary, Canada, 7 July 1930
**Rangers career:** 1950 to 1961
**Appearances and goals:**

| League | | FA Cup | | Lg Cup | | Europe | |
|---|---|---|---|---|---|---|---|
| A | G | A | G | A | G | A | G |
| 178 | 1 | 32 | 0 | 55 | 0 | 10 | 0 |

*Total appearances:* 275
*Total goals:* 1
**League Championships:** 1952-53; 1955-56
**Scottish Cup:** 1952-53; 1959-60
**Honours:** 1 Scotland cap

Despite full-back John Little being born in Calgary, Canada, he came to

Scotland as a boy, and after first attending a rugby-playing school, started to play football at Queen's Park Senior Secondary—a famous football nursery.

Having represented Scotland at schoolboy international level, he joined Queen's Park and not long after became an amateur international. His form for Queen's Park attracted the attention of a number of top clubs north of the border, and it came as no surprise when he opted for Rangers, turning professional with the Ibrox club in the summer of 1951.

Making his Rangers debut at right-back in a goalless draw at East Fife in a League Cup match, he soon switched to the opposite flank and became the perfect successor to Jock Shaw. He missed just two games in his first season at the club as Rangers finished the campaign as runners-up to Hibernian in the League and went down 3-2 to Dundee in the League Cup Final.

The following season he helped Rangers win the League Championship on goal difference from their great rivals of the day, Hibernian, and to success in the Scottish Cup, where a Billy Simpson goal was enough to defeat Aberdeen.

Little, who had represented the Scottish League, was given his full international debut in May 1953 in place of his team-mate Sammy Cox against Sweden, but the Scots went down 2-1. The following season, Rangers slipped down to fourth place in the League, but Little scored what proved to be his only goal for the club in a 1-1 draw at bottom club Hamilton Academical.

There was a strong similarity in the playing styles of John Little and the club's previous left-back, 'Tiger' Shaw. His sheer speed, energy and enthusiasm saw him occupy the No.3 shirt for nine seasons, although injuries ruled him out for much of the 1958-59 campaign. Few wingers in the Scottish League could get past John Little, and if they did, he would invariably catch them! He was an all-action type, strong in the tackle and with effective distribution skills.

One of only a handful of Rangers players to have been capped for Scotland who have been born outside the country, his charm and even temperament endeared him to all Rangers fans as he went on to make 275 appearances in his time at Ibrox.

A qualified Physical Education teacher, he moved on to Morton in the summer of 1962 and eventually taught in a school in Greenock.

## PETER LOVENKRANDS

**Born:** Horsholm, Denmark, 29 January 1980
**Rangers career:** 2000 to 2006
**Appearances and goals:**

| League | | FA Cup | | Lg Cup | | Europe | |
|---|---|---|---|---|---|---|---|
| A | G | A | G | A | G | A | G |
| 89/39 | 38 | 7/2 | 5 | 10/2 | 4 | 23/4 | 8 |

Total appearances: 129/47
Total goals: 55
**League Championships:** 2002-03; 2004-05
**Scottish Cup:** 2001-02
**League Cup:** 2001-02; 2002-03
**Honours:** 18 Denmark caps

Danish international Peter Lovenkrands signed for Rangers in the summer of 2000 in a £1.5 million deal from AB Copenhagen, although it was the 2001-02 season when he first came to prominence, culminating in him scoring two goals in the Scottish Cup Final victory over Celtic.

Alongside future Danish international Martin Albrechtsen, Lovenkrands was called up for the Danish Under-19 national team in September 1997, and they both signed their first professional contracts with Superliga club Akademisk Boldklub (AB Copenhagen) in February 1998. Lovenkrands made his Superliga debut in July 1998 and was quickly touted as a future Danish international by AB manager Christian Andersen. He scored five goals in eight games for the Danish Under-19 side and was named 1998 Danish Under-19 Player of the Year. He was part of the 1999 Danish Cup-winning team, though he did not play in the final against Aalborg BK because of injury.

Having joined Rangers, the pacy forward, who can also play on the wing, made his debut as a substitute in a 4-1 home win over Dunfermline Athletic. The majority of his appearances that season were from the bench and, in fact, his only league start came in a 1-0 defeat at Hibernian.

It was a different story in 2001-02, as he helped Rangers to success in both the domestic cup competitions. Having beaten Ayr United 4-0 to lift the League Cup, Rangers met Celtic in the Scottish Cup Final. It was a tense and exciting game, with a John Hartson header giving the Hoops an early lead. Two minutes later, Lovenkrands spun the Celtic defence to drill home a low left-foot shot from the edge of the box. Despite Rangers having most of the game, Celtic went ahead early in the second-half before Barry Ferguson levelled the scores with a delightful free-kick over the wall. With the game deep in injury time and the referee poised to blow his whistle for full-time, McCann floated in a perfect cross which was well met by Lovenkrands for a deserved winner.

In the close season, both Barcelona and Inter Milan inquired about the services of the Danish international, but thankfully he opted to stay at Ibrox. In 2002-03 he scored 10 goals in 21 starts as Rangers won the League Championship, and scored one of the goals in the League Cup Final as Celtic were beaten 2-1. Despite a hit-and-miss season because of injuries during the 2003-04 campaign, Lovenkrands was called up to the Danish squad for Euro 2004, but only played in the quarter-final defeat to the Czech Republic.

Though Rangers won the League title again in 2004–05, Lovenkrands' contribution was less successful, and in the close season he trialled for Premiership side Middlesbrough. In the end, however, he decided not to move to the Riverside. Remaining at Ibrox for the 2005–06 season, Lovenkrands continued for the most part to be played out of position on the left-wing rather than his preferred position of centre-forward. He did, though, have his most successful season, his total of 14 League goals including a hat-trick in a 3-2 defeat of Kilmarnock.

He also played an important role in Rangers' run to the last 16 of the Champions League, scoring four goals. In the group stage he opened the scoring in the 3-2 win over FC Porto, and with his goal in the 1-1 draw against Inter Milan he secured Rangers advancement to the knock-out round. When through to the last 16 he scored in both legs of the game against Villareal FC, but unfortunately Rangers were eliminated on the away goal rule.

After six years at Ibrox, his contract expired, and in the summer of 2006 he left the club on a free transfer. Reportedly in talks with a number of clubs including AS Roma and Spanish side Osasuna, he eventually signed for German side FC Schalke 04. His form for the German side brought him a recall to the Danish national team.

## STUART McCALL

**Born:** Leeds, 10 June 1964
**Rangers career:** 1991 to 1998
**Appearances and goals:**

| League | | FA Cup | | Lg Cup | | Europe | |
|---|---|---|---|---|---|---|---|
| A | G | A | G | A | G | A | G |
| 186/8 | 15 | 25/2 | 0 | 15/1 | 3 | 28 | 2 |

Total appearances: 254/11
Total goals: 20
**League Championships:** 1991-92; 1992-93; 1993-94; 1994-95; 1995-96
**Scottish Cup:** 1991-92; 1992-93; 1995-96
**League Cup:** 1992-93; 1993-94
**Honours:** 40 Scotland caps

It is perhaps fitting that Stuart McCall was born in Leeds, given that he appeared to have modelled his style on that great Elland Road Scot of the seventies, Billy Bremner. A tenacious tackler, McCall exemplified the superb will to win which ensured Rangers continued their domination of the domestic game in Scotland during his time with the club.

McCall started his career with Bradford City, and it didn't take long for the little man with the red hair to become a big star there. It was at

Valley Parade that McCall received his first international recognition, being selected for England at Under-21 level. Thankfully for both Scotland and Rangers, he did not play for the young English, although he came extremely close, as he was on the bench.

It was also at Bradford that he endured his worst memory in football, the fire disaster which plunged British soccer into mourning in 1985. A move to a big club seemed inevitable, and in the summer of 1988 he joined Everton for a fee of £850,000. However, McCall strangely failed to really establish himself at Goodison, and it is worth remembering that his finest moment there—two goals in the 3-2 FA Cup Final defeat against Liverpool—was achieved as a substitute!

The departure of Trevor Steven for his multi-million deal to Marseille in August 1991 paved the way for McCall's arrival at Ibrox. He quickly established himself as a fixture in the team—the perfect workhorse in midfield, as well as an accomplished wide midfielder and on occasion a more than competent right-back. Indeed, his willingness to play anywhere resulted in him wearing every outfield shirt at Ibrox bar one—the No.11 shirt occupied for much of his time at the club by Brian Laudrup.

His career highlights with Rangers were many and varied, and included five League Championship successes, but a goal against Aberdeen in the 1992-93 Skol Cup Final was a crucial one and paved the way for an eventual 2-1 success. Although he had more than his fair share of injuries during his time at Ibrox, he proved himself a relentless competitor whose ebullient nature off the pitch accurately reflected his dynamism on it.

He became a valued member of the Scottish national side, and will be long remembered for a crucial goal against Sweden in the 1990 World Cup Finals. At Euro '96 there was barely a better performer for Scotland.

McCall left Rangers to return to Bradford City in the summer of 1998. Given a three-year contract and appointed captain, he won the club's Player of the Year award in his first season back at Valley Parade. In the summer of 2000 he was appointed assistant to City manager Chris Hutchings, and when Hutchings was sacked, took over as caretaker-manager. One of Bradford City's all-time greats, he had scored 55 goals in 454 games before leaving to join Sheffield United as player-coach. In April 2002, McCall's testimonial match against Rangers attracted over 21,000 to Valley Parade.

A key member of the Blades' side, his energetic displays brought out the best in the younger midfielders around him. Having coached the reserves to the League title, he hung up his boots for the last time and became assistant-manager at Sheffield United under Neil Warnock. He left Bramall Lane following the Blades' relegation and is now back at Bradford City as manager.

# NEIL McCANN

**Born:** Greenock, 11 August 1974
**Rangers career:** 1998 to 2003
**Appearances and goals:**

| League | | FA Cup | | Lg Cup | | Europe | |
|--------|---|--------|---|--------|---|--------|---|
| **A** | **G** | **A** | **G** | **A** | **G** | **A** | **G** |
| 66/47 | 20 | 17/4 | 3 | 6/1 | 0 | 12/16 | 3 |

*Total appearances:* 101/68
*Total goals:* 26
**League Championships:** 1998-99; 1999-2000; 2002-03
**Scottish Cup:** 1998-99; 1999-2000; 2001-02; 2002-03
**League Cup:** 2001-02
**Honours:** 26 Scotland caps

Only the second born Catholic after Mo Johnston to play for Rangers in modern times, Neil McCann arrived at Ibrox in December 1998 when manager Dick Advocaat paid Hearts £2 million for his services.

McCann started his career with Dundee before moving on to Hearts in 1996. He ended his first season at the club with an appearance in the League Cup Final, but Hearts lost 4-3 to Rangers in a seven-goal thriller. The following season he had his best-ever campaign in terms of goals scored, with 10 in 35 outings. He also helped Hearts win the Scottish Cup Final with a 2-1 defeat of Rangers—the Tynecastle club's first trophy in 36 years!

He had impressed the Ibrox club's management team so much that they secured his signature midway through the following campaign.

He had made his international debut for Scotland just a couple of months before he joined Rangers as a late substitute for Ally McCoist in a goalless draw in Lithuania. His first appearance in a starting line-up came in March 1999 against the Czech Republic. He scored in consecutive matches in September 2003 during the qualifying rounds for Euro 2004.

Towards the end of his first season at Ibrox, McCann famously scored two goals in a 3-0 win over arch-rivals Celtic at Parkhead, to clinch the SPL title. During five seasons with Rangers, McCann suffered more than his fair share of injuries, but throughout his stay, he remained an important member of the Light Blues' squad.

Having beaten Celtic 1-0 to win the Scottish Cup in 1998-99, McCann helped the club retain both trophies the following season—Rangers finishing 21 points clear of runners-up Celtic and beating Aberdeen 4-0 in the Scottish Cup Final. Though he came off the bench in the final the following season to win his only League Cup winners' medal, his hat-trick in a 5-0 defeat of Kilmarnock was not enough to inspire Rangers to success in the League.

In Rangers' seventh treble-winning season of 2002-03, McCann struggled with injuries and failed to appear in the League Cup Final. Although many of his 169 appearances in all competitions were from the bench, McCann was still a highly regarded first team squad member when Alex McLeish allowed him to join Southampton in a £1.5 million deal.

Unfortunately a series of injuries made it difficult for him to maintain his place in the south coast club's team, and in January 2006 he rejoined his former club Hearts after his contract with Southampton was terminated by mutual consent. He sustained a serious injury while playing in his first match following his return, but later returned to action in the Champions' League qualifier against Siroki Brijeg of Bosnia. Sadly, he then suffered a double leg break during Hearts' 5-0 defeat by Celtic.

## JOHN McCLELLAND

**Born:** Belfast, 7 December 1955
**Rangers career:** 1981 to 1985
**Appearances and goals:**

| League | | FA Cup | | Lg Cup | | Europe | |
|---|---|---|---|---|---|---|---|
| A | G | A | G | A | G | A | G |
| 96 | 4 | 13 | 1 | 30 | 2 | 14 | 1 |

*Total appearances:* 153
*Total goals:* 8
**League Cup:** 1983-84; 1984-85
**Honours:** 53 Northern Ireland caps

Many times capped Northern Ireland international defender John McClelland, who had played with Portadown in Ireland, Cardiff City in Wales and came from Mansfield Town in England to Rangers, had a unique four-country career record when he arrived at Ibrox for a fee of £100,000 in May 1981.

Having started his career in his native Ireland with Portadown, he tried his luck in the Football League with Cardiff City, and though he played a handful of games in the 1974-75 season, League football had come too early for the young McClelland and he joined Bangor City.

Mansfield Town gave him a second chance at League level, and it was while he was at Field Mill that his career took off in a big way when Scottish giants Rangers took him north of the border.

Rangers manager John Greig took the 6ft 2in McClelland on a summer tour of Sweden prior to the start of the 1981-82 season, where he played initially at left-back. Unfortunately an ankle injury on that tour dogged his early days with the club. He made his Rangers debut in a League Cup tie at Raith Rovers, a match Rangers won 3-1, but found himself in and out of the side as injuries took their toll.

In 1982-83 he helped Rangers reach both cup finals, but each time was on the losing side, going down 1-0 to Aberdeen in the Scottish Cup and 2-1 to arch rivals Celtic in the League Cup. The following season Rangers again finished fourth in the League, but McClelland picked up his first medal as Celtic were defeated 3-2—courtesy of an Ally McCoist hat-trick—in the League Cup Final. In 1984-85, his last season with the club, Rangers retained the trophy by beating Dundee 1-0, Ian Ferguson scoring the game's only goal.

During his best days at Ibrox, John McClelland was certainly one of the best defensive footballers in Britain. Rangers fans were genuinely sad to see him leave the club following a dispute over money with manager Jock Wallace. He was transferred to Watford, the Vicarage Road club paying £225,000 for his services.

McClelland played in Northern Ireland's 1982 and 1986 World Cup final teams and represented the Football League against the Rest of the World at Wembley in August 1987. In the summer of 1989 he joined Leeds United, but struggled with injury in his time at Elland Road, and was loaned to his former club Watford. Despite these injuries, he managed his final appearance for Northern Ireland, playing in the 3-2 home defeat by Norway in March 1990.

After a loan spell with Notts County, McClelland joined St Johnstone as player-coach, later being elevated to player-manager. After losing his job with the Saints he turned out briefly for Carrick Rangers, before having spells with Arbroath, Wycombe Wanderers and Yeovil Town. McClelland then had a brief spell as assistant-manger to Chris Kamara at Bradford City before linking up with Darlington as player-coach. Having made just one appearance for the Quakers, he tragically broke his leg at Hartlepool.

Having finally decided to end his playing career, he was assistant-manager at Leeds United for a spell, and has remained at Elland Road as the Yorkshire club's Tours and PR Manager.

# PETER McCLOY

**Born:** Girvan, 16 November 1946
**Rangers career:** 1970 to 1986
**Appearances and goals:**

| League | | FA Cup | | Lg Cup | | Europe | |
|---|---|---|---|---|---|---|---|
| **A** | **G** | **A** | **G** | **A** | **G** | **A** | **G** |
| 351 | 0 | 55 | 0 | 86 | 0 | 43 | 0 |

*Total appearances:* 535
*Total goals:* 0
**League Championships:** 1975-76
**Scottish Cup:** 1972-73; 1975-76; 1977-78; 1978-79
**League Cup:** 1970-71; 1978-79; 1983-84; 1984-85
**European Cup Winners Cup:** 1971-72
**Honours:** 4 Scotland caps

The towering presence of Rangers' longest-serving goalkeeper Peter McCloy and his birthplace on the Ayrshire coast gave him the nickname 'The Girvan Lighthouse'.

From a goalkeeping family—his father had kept goal for St Mirren—he started out with Crosshill Thistle before signing for Motherwell in 1963. Though he saw off the challenge of Alan Wyllie, he fared less well against Keith MacRae, despite the latter's insistence on playing outfield whenever possible! McCloy won a Summer Cup medal in 1965 and his displays en route to the final success over Dundee United were excellent given his youth. He represented the Scottish League against both the Irish Leagues, while at Fir Park McCloy was actually languishing in Motherwell's reserves when he was exchanged for Bobby Watson and Brian Heron in order for him to begin his Rangers career.

He was on the beaten side on his debut as Rangers went down 2-1 to Dunfermline Athletic and conceded another two on his next outing against Dundee. But for the next four seasons, he made the position his own, winning his first medal when he kept a clean sheet in the 1-0 League Cup Final win over Celtic.

The following season he took a more active role in the club's success in the European Cup Winners' Cup Final against Moscow Dynamo. One of the mightiest of kickers, his downfield clearances became an attacking option for Rangers. It was a long kick from the long man that found Willie Johnston in position to score Rangers' third goal in the 3-2 thriller in Barcelona.

When Stewart Kennedy joined Rangers the following year, McCloy was forced to share the goalkeeping duties with the former Stenhousemuir keeper before reverting to becoming first choice again in 1978, although he was between the posts for the 1973 Scottish Cup Final when Rangers defeated arch-rivals Celtic by the same scoreline as in Barcelona.

Having helped Rangers win the League Championship in 1975-76, he never missed a game in the double-winning campaign of 1978-79 as Rangers won both domestic cup competitions. He held his place in the Rangers side until the arrival of Jim Stewart in March 1981, though again his durability won the day.

In international terms, McCloy was a contemporary with Alistair Hunter of Kilmarnock and Celtic, David Harvey of Leeds United, Bobby Clark of Aberdeen and later Alan Rough of Partick Thistle—all formidable opponents— and so he only represented the national side on four occasions.

Following the arrival of Graeme Souness and Chris Woods in 1986, McCloy, who had played in a total of 535 games, became a coach at Ibrox and subsequently became a freelance coach, working with Hearts and a number of other clubs.

# ALLY McCOIST

**Born:** Bellshill, 24 September 1962
**Rangers career:** 1983 to 1998
**Appearances and goals:**

| League | | FA Cup | | Lg Cup | | Europe | |
|---|---|---|---|---|---|---|---|
| **A** | **G** | **A** | **G** | **A** | **G** | **A** | **G** |
| 331/57 | 243 | 35/8 | 25 | 45/7 | 45 | 42/9 | 21 |

*Total appearances:* 453/81

*Total goals:* 334

**League Championships:** 1986-87; 1988-89; 1989-90; 1990-91; 1991-92; 1992-93; 1993-94; 1995-96; 1996-97

**Scottish Cup:** 1991-92

**League Cup:** 1984-85; 1986-87; 1987-88; 1988-89; 1992-93; 1993-94; 1996-97

**Honours:** 61 Scotland caps

Rangers' all-time leading scorer, extrovert and crowd favourite, Ally McCoist actually needed three invitations to join Rangers before finally making the move in 1983. He holds the club record for League and European goals, was the first Scottish player to win the Golden Boot and then promptly retained it. He was also the club's leading scorer in nine of his 15 seasons as a Light Blue.

Signed by John Greig in June 1983 for £175,000 from Sunderland, McCoist is one of those rare individuals who turned down Ibrox once, before getting another opportunity to join the fold. On leaving St Johnstone a couple of seasons previously, the youngster had opted to try his luck down south with the Wearside club and declined Greig's advances. Both club and player have had good reason to be grateful for his change of mind shortly after.

He was not welcomed rapturously by Rangers fans, who were well aware of history and questioned his commitment to the Ibrox club. His first couple of seasons with Rangers were difficult, but McCoist was determined to succeed and his eventual success at club level was rewarded with the first of 61 caps when in April 1986 he played against Holland. Sadly, his record of 19 goals for his country didn't come close to his club statistics.

His early misses in those first couple of seasons were indicative of the poor Rangers team he was playing in, but it was a temporary lapse and he soon became the hero of the Rangers faithful.

His highest total of goals in the League season was 34, a total he achieved three times, in 1986-87, 1991-92 and 1992-93. He also scored no fewer than 28 hat-tricks, with a highest of five in a season which he achieved twice. His best individual haul in a match was netting all four goals against Falkirk in October 1992.

He is second in the all-time list of Rangers scorers in Old Firm games with a total of 27. The player who holds the record is R.C. Hamilton, who hit his 35 around the turn of the nineteenth century.

*Ally McCoist holds aloft the League Cup, after Rangers beat Celtic in the 1984 final (www.snspix.com)*

Ally McCoist was often at his best in a crowded penalty area, snapping up half-chances. But not only did he have the knack of being in the right place at the right time, he also scored more than his fair share of spectacular goals. Reading the game well, the secret of his finishing was his great anticipation, which allowed him to snap up chances before opposition defenders had realised the danger.

Though he flourished during the early days of Graeme Souness's reign with vital strikes against Celtic and in Cup Finals, his personality seemed to clash with the Rangers boss, and he found himself on the bench for much of the 1990-91 season, earning himself the nickname 'The Judge'.

When Walter Smith took over, McCoist went on to become an even greater Rangers striker. He and Mark Hateley formed a phenomenal strike partnership that produced 101 goals.

Sadly, he broke his leg playing for Scotland in Portugal in 1993, and though he had already scored 34 league goals, he missed the opportunity of setting a new personal high. He did bounce back to score a sensational overhead winner in the following season's League Cup Final against Hibernian, after coming off the bench.

At the tail end of 1994 his contribution to Scottish football and Rangers was recognised as he picked up an MBE at Buckingham Palace. His scoring feats alone dictate that he will be remembered as one of Scotland's greatest-ever marksmen. His last match for Rangers was in the 1998 Scottish Cup Final. Fittingly he scored, but the competition was never his luckiest and he finished on the losing side as Hearts ran out winners 2-1.

He left Ibrox that summer to play for Kilmarnock, and his first full start for his new club saw him score a hat-trick against Hearts. In the crowd that day was then Scotland manager Craig Brown, who having left him out of the '98 World Cup party for France, asked him to play for Scotland again! His last first-class game was on 20 May 2001 when he helped Kilmarnock beat Celtic 1-0, after which he has become an accomplished television personality.

Having assisted Walter Smith with the Scottish national team and helped them top their group for qualification for the finals of Euro 2008, he sensationally returned to Rangers in January 2007 as assistant-manager to Smith.

## IAN McCOLL

**Born:** Alexandria, 7 June 1927
**Rangers career:** 1946 to 1960
**Appearances and goals:**

| League | | FA Cup | | Lg Cup | | Europe | |
|---|---|---|---|---|---|---|---|
| A | G | A | G | A | G | A | G |
| 360 | 11 | 59 | 1 | 100 | 2 | 7 | 0 |

*Total appearances:* 526
*Total goals:* 14
**League Championships:** 1946-47; 1948-49; 1949-50; 1952-53; 1955-56; 1956-57
**Scottish Cup:** 1947-48; 1948-49; 1949-50; 1952-53; 1959-60
**League Cup:** 1946-47; 1948-49;
**Honours:** 14 Scotland caps

Wing-half Ian McColl became captain of Rangers in the 1950s, and can comfortably lay claim to being one of the Ibrox club's greatest-ever servants.

Hailing from the Vale of Leven, McColl, after local school and Boys' Brigade, was playing for Queen's Park when he was 16 and was signed by Rangers before he had turned 18. McColl spent a season and a half or so in the club's reserves to acclimatise him to the world of professional football, before making his League debut in a 2-1 home win over Morton in November 1946.

He was the final piece in the club's legendary Iron Curtain defence which was so effective in Rangers' considerable successes of the period. He ended his first season with the club with a League Championship medal and a League Cup winners' medal after Rangers had beaten Aberdeen 4-0 in the final.

McColl was tall, very athletic, a powerful tackler and ball winner who would fight for every ball and battle throughout the entire ninety minutes. In a 10-year period, other teams averaged less than a goal a game against Rangers, which again is indicative of just how strong the club's defence was.

During his time at Ibrox, McColl was to win a host of domestic honours— six League Championship medals and successes in five Scottish Cup Finals and two League Cup Finals. One of his best displays in a Rangers shirt came in the 1960 Scottish Cup Final against Kilmarnock. Recalled to the side following a long absence, he replaced the injured Harold Davis. He was totally committed, and his excellent passing skills set up both his side's goals, scored by Jimmy Millar in a 2-0 win.

McColl, who appeared in 526 games for Rangers, was still turning out for the club when he was appointed manager of Scotland. Though he didn't have sole charge of the national side—the SFA picked the teams and also had a great say in the tactics—the results were indifferent, with the best results being a 6-2 win in Spain and 2-1 defeat of England at Wembley. Both these results came in the summer of 1963.

Within a month of leaving his post with the national side, he was appointed manager of Sunderland. He spent £340,000 on new players, including Jim Baxter from his former club and Neil Martin from Hibernian, but they rarely showed good form. The club just avoided relegation to Division Two, and disappointing results the following season led to McColl, who was a qualified engineer, having gained his BSc at Edinburgh University, parting company with the Wearsiders.

## ALEX MacDONALD

**Born:** Glasgow, 17 March 1948
**Rangers career:** 1968 to 1980

**Appearances and goals:**

| League | | FA Cup | | Lg Cup | | Europe | |
|---|---|---|---|---|---|---|---|
| **A** | **G** | **A** | **G** | **A** | **G** | **A** | **G** |
| 320/17 | 51 | 46/4 | 15 | 75/4 | 18 | 37/1 | 10 |

*Total appearances:* 478/26

*Total goals:* 94

**League Championships:** 1974-75; 1975-76; 1977-78

**Scottish Cup:** 1972-73; 1975-76; 1977-78; 1978-79

**League Cup:** 1970-71; 1975-76; 1977-78; 1978-79

**European Cup Winners' Cup:** 1971-72

**Honours:** 1 Scotland cap

One of the club's most valuable signings, competitive midfielder Alex MacDonald arrived at Ibrox in November 1968 after Rangers' manager David White paid St Johnstone £50,000 for his services.

Though he took a little time to settle and initially struggled to win over the Rangers fans, MacDonald went on to become a firm favourite as he consistently demonstrated his great passion for the Light Blues' cause. Playing on both the left-hand side of midfield or at inside-forward, MacDonald became the powerhouse of a Rangers side that was hugely successful throughout the seventies.

Dubbed 'Doddie' by the Rangers faithful, he was most adept at stealing into the blind side of opposing defences and snatching vital goals. During

*Alex MacDonald heads the goal that puts Rangers 1-0 up against Juventus in the 1978 European Champions' Cup (www.snspix.com)*

Rangers' European Cup Winners Cup success of 1971-72, MacDonald struck the solitary goal in the first round home tie win over Rennes, and later repeated the feat in the quarter-final defeat of Italian side Torino. But perhaps his most important goal came in the 1975 Scottish League Cup Final against Celtic, when he fulfilled a boyhood dream by scoring the winning goal with a dramatic diving header.

His form for Rangers around this time won him full international honours for Scotland, when he played in a 1-0 win over Switzerland at Hampden Park. Though not the most prolific of scorers, he did net in another final in 1977-78 as the Gers beat Aberdeen 2-1 to lift the Scottish Cup.

In a Rangers career spanning over 12 years, MacDonald appeared in over 500 games for the club, winning three League Championship medals and four Scottish Cup and League Cup winners' medals. A vital member of Jock Wallace's treble-winning sides of 1975-76 and 1977-78, his European Cup Winners' Cup glory is a fitting reward for such a dedicated professional.

A player of total commitment, he was allowed to leave Rangers in 1980 and joined Hearts for a fee of £30,000. He took over the Tynecastle club's captaincy, but even he couldn't stem the tide and the Jam Tarts finished bottom of the Premier League and were relegated.

In January 1982 he was appointed player-manager, and though Hearts missed out on promotion by one point, he was slowly turning things around and they secured promotion back to the top flight the following season. Eventually deciding to hang up his boots and concentrate on management, he took the Tynecastle club into Europe in 1984, and two years later secured the Manager of the Year award after taking the club to the verge of the Premiership title. After taking Hearts to runners-up in 1987-88 and third the season after, he was sacked in 1990 after the 3-1 home defeat by Rangers!

He later went on to success with Airdrie, taking them to two Scottish Cup Finals in 1992 and 1995 and to runners-up spot in the First Division in 1996-97.

## RONNIE McKINNON

**Born:** Glasgow, 20 August 1940
**Rangers career:** 1960 to 1973
**Appearances and goals:**

| League | | FA Cup | | Lg Cup | | Europe | |
|---|---|---|---|---|---|---|---|
| A | G | A | G | A | G | A | G |
| 301 | 2 | 44 | 0 | 83 | 0 | 45 | 1 |

*Total appearances:* 473
*Total goals:* 3
**League Championships:** 1962-63; 1963-64
**Scottish Cup:** 1961-62; 1962-63; 1963-64; 1965-66

**League Cup:** 1963-64; 1964-65; 1970-71
**Honours:** 28 Scotland caps

There is little doubt that Ronnie McKinnon was the best centre-half Rangers had had since Willie Woodburn. A product of Benburb, the local Govan junior team, and of Dunipace Juniors, he had outstanding pace, great composure and tremendous authority.

When he arrived at Ibrox, he was a wing-half, but it wasn't long before he was converted into a centre-half. When he came into the Rangers side, he was considered nothing more than a stop-gap, deputising for the injured Baillie and Paterson, but he developed into an international class defender. However, early in his career, he was criticised for being weak in the air, and his lack of height for a central defender saw Spurs take full advantage in a European Cup Winners Cup match at White Hart Lane by beating Rangers 5-2.

Throughout most of the sixties, he shared the Scotland No.5 shirt with Celtic's Billy McNeill, going on to win 28 caps and playing in the side that beat world champions England 3-2 at Wembley in 1967.

A well-rounded footballer, McKinnon had a most calming effect on the Rangers defence. Comfortable on the ball, he never seemed under pressure, and the half-back line of Greig, McKinnon and Baxter was one of the finest at both club and international level.

Though the events of 3 November 1971 will be remembered as some of the most remarkable in the club's history, for Ronnie McKinnon, it was the day his Rangers dream died! Having beaten Sporting Lisbon 3-2 at Ibrox in the first leg of the European Cup Winners Cup second round tie, Rangers went down 4-3 after extra-time to Sporting in the Jose Alvalade Stadium. With the tie having finished at 6-6, Dutch referee Laruens van Raavens incorrectly ordered a penalty shoot-out. Rangers missed four of their five spot-kicks and the Portuguese celebrated what they thought was a dramatic victory.

Rangers boss Willie Waddell checked his rule book after being told that extra-time goals count double in the event of a level aggregate score. The referee had forgotten that the rule had been changed that summer and so the penalty shoot-out verdict was overturned. Rangers were declared the winners, and of course went on to win the trophy in Barcelona the following May. But while his team-mates and Rangers fans celebrated wildly, McKinnon's world collapsed around him. He suffered a double fracture of his right leg and never played for the Light Blues again.

Devastated to have his career curtailed at the age of only 31, he was allowed to leave Ibrox and moved to South Africa where he made a brief comeback playing for Durban United. He then moved to Australia, where he became a car salesman, but is now back in his native Scotland, residing in Lewis.

# GEORGE McLEAN

**Born:** Paisley, 26 May 1943
**Rangers career:** 1962 to 1967
**Appearances and goals:**

| League | | FA Cup | | Lg Cup | | Europe | |
|---|---|---|---|---|---|---|---|
| A | G | A | G | A | G | A | G |
| 69 | 49 | 14 | 8 | 28 | 23 | 6 | 2 |

*Total appearances:* 117
*Total goals:* 82
**League Championships:** 1963-64
**Scottish Cup:** 1963-64; 1965-66
**Honours:** 1 Scotland cap

George 'Dandy' McLean was without doubt one of the most enigmatic and controversial players ever to wear the light blue of Rangers FC. Originally a wing-half, he forced himself on the attention of the Ibrox club when playing against Rangers for St Mirren in the 1962 Scottish Cup Final, a match the Gers won 2-0.

McLean signed for Rangers for a then record fee between Scottish clubs of £26,500 in January 1963. Playing equally as well at inside-forward, it was thought he would make the ideal successor to Ian McMillan, although he was a completely different type of player.

He was indeed a 'dandy'—a sharp dresser, a driver of quality cars and certainly enjoyed life to the full away from the pressures of the game! Rangers manager Scot Symon had some problems in trying to control him, but there was nothing malicious in it at all.

Symon moved him to play alongside Jim Forrest in the Rangers forward line, and was rewarded with a hatful of goals. He helped Rangers win the 1963-64 League Championship, scoring 10 goals in 19 games, including his first hat-trick for the club in a 4-0 home win over Falkirk.

In 1965-66 he scored 39 goals in 34 games, including 25 in 24 league outings. This total included hat-tricks in the defeats of Kilmarnock (5-0 at home) and St Johnstone (3-0 away). McLean netted his third treble that season in the Scottish Cup as Airdrie were beaten 5-0 in the first round of the competition. He also scored 10 minutes from the end of the Scottish Cup semi-final against Aberdeen to put Rangers in the final, but then missed the final. He played in the final replay, helping Rangers to a 1-0 win over Celtic.

McLean's last game for Rangers came in January 1967, when he and his fellow strike partner Jim Forrest were held to be the guilty men responsible for the infamous Rangers Scottish Cup defeat at the hands of Berwick Rangers. There is no doubt about it, the Ibrox club were certainly paranoid about that result!

McLean left Ibrox and joined Dundee in exchange for Andy Penman. He helped the Fir Park club reach the 1968 League Cup Final, where they lost 5-3 to Celtic in one of the competition's most exciting finals.

George McLean later played for Dunfermline Athletic, Ayr United and Hamilton Academical before going to work for a double glazing company.

## TOMMY McLEAN

**Born:** Ashgill, 2 June 1947
**Rangers career:** 1971 to 1982
**Appearances and goals:**

| League | | FA Cup | | Lg Cup | | Europe | |
|---|---|---|---|---|---|---|---|
| **A** | **G** | **A** | **G** | **A** | **G** | **A** | **G** |
| 274/24 | 35 | 43/3 | 12 | 66/4 | 8 | 30/1 | 5 |

*Total appearances:* 413/32
*Total goals:* 60
**League Championships:** 1974-75; 1975-76; 1977-78
**Scottish Cup:** 1972-73; 1975-76; 1977-78; 1978-79
**League Cup:** 1975-76; 1977-78; 1978-79
**European Cup Winners Cup:** 1971-72
**Honours:** 6 Scotland caps

Tommy McLean was one of the most intelligent and perceptive players ever to pull on the light blue jersey for Rangers, and followed a sequence of outstanding right-wingers—Willie Waddell, Alex Scott, Willie Henderson. Indeed, McLean might even be considered the greatest of them all.

He began his career by signing for Kilmarnock, managed by Willie Waddell, after his father had persuaded him to turn down Rangers' Scot Symon and put pen to paper for the Rugby Park club. When he did join Rangers, they too were managed by Willie Waddell! During his time with Killie, he played in one of the club's greatest-ever games. Having been beaten 3-0 in Germany by Eintracht Frankfurt and then gone further behind in the return leg, he inspired his side to a marvellous 5-4 aggregate win with a 5-1 victory on the night. Named Man of the Match, he actually made his League debut against Dunfermline Athletic four days later!

Having won representative honours for the Scottish League, he won his first full cap for Scotland in October 1968, but by the time he made the last of his six international appearances, he had joined Rangers for a fee of £65,000.

In his first season at Ibrox, McLean replaced Willie Henderson and helped the club to success in that season's European Cup Winners' Cup as Rangers beat Moscow Dynamo 3-2 in the final. A member of the Rangers side that lifted the Scottish Cup the following season, he netted his first hat-trick for the club in the 1973-74 League Cup when Queen's Park were demolished 8-0. His best season in terms of goals scored was the club's League Championship-winning season of 1974-75, when his total of 14 included another treble in a 5-1 win at Dumbarton.

McLean was wonderfully astute and tactically aware, and played an influential role as captain in the club's treble-winning seasons of 1975-76 and 1977-78.

He retired after the Scottish Cup Final of 1982 to become coach and assistant-manager to John Greig at Ibrox. When Greig parted company with the club in October 1983, McLean managed the team and did it very well until Jock Wallace arrived to take over the reins.

He became part-time manager of Morton, before in the summer of 1984, being appointed manager of Motherwell. He led the Steelmen to a First Division Championship win in 1984-85 and to success in the Scottish Cup in 1991. He left Motherwell after a disagreement, and after a short time managed Hearts. On leaving Tynecastle he had a brief spell with Raith Rovers before managing Dundee United. Though he led the Tannadice club to the Coca Cola Cup Final of 1997, he left less than a year later following a series of poor results.

McLean, who had enjoyed successful managerial stints at most of his clubs, also had a spell at Ibrox coaching Rangers' Under-19 side.

## IAN McMILLAN

**Born:** Airdrie, 18 March 1931
**Rangers career:** 1958 to 1964
**Appearances and goals:**

| League | | FA Cup | | Lg Cup | | Europe | |
|---|---|---|---|---|---|---|---|
| **A** | **G** | **A** | **G** | **A** | **G** | **A** | **G** |
| 127 | 36 | 23 | 6 | 22 | 6 | 22 | 7 |

*Total appearances:* 194
*Total goals:* 55
**League Championships:** 1958-59; 1960-61
**Scottish Cup:** 1959-60; 1961-62; 1962-63
**League Cup:** 1960-61; 1961-62
**Honours:** 6 Scotland caps

Ian McMillan was dubbed the 'Wee Prime Minister' because of his control of affairs and in recognition of the then Prime Minister Harold Macmillan. He was an old-style inside-forward and one of the club's players of the highest class.

McMillan started out with his home-town club Airdrie, and during a decade of international football with them, won full international honours for Scotland. He joined Rangers in October 1958 and made his debut against Raith Rovers, scoring his new side's first and last goals in a most entertaining 4-4 draw. The Ibrox club had been having an indifferent spell of form, but from that match on, with McMillan in the side, they lost just one of their next 23 matches. He ended his first season with eight goals in 26 games, helping Rangers win the League Championship.

Not a prolific scorer, his best season in terms of goals scored was 1959-60, when he netted 14 goals in 27 league games as Rangers finished third behind Hearts and Kilmarnock.

With the arrival of Jim Baxter in the summer of 1960, one of the great Rangers inside-forward partnerships was in place. Protected by his right-half Harold Davis, McMillan was the classic Scottish inside-forward. He was technically skilled, possessed great ball control and clever dribbling skills, and along with Baxter was instrumental in the club's successes of the early sixties. Neither of those players was much concerned with defence, and McMillan in particular was outstanding in feeding his outside-right and releasing the speedy strikers Ralph Brand and Jimmy Millar.

During the course of the 1962-63 season, Rangers reached the Scottish FA Cup Final where their opponents were Celtic. It was the first Old Firm final since 1928, and with Brand scoring Rangers' goal, ended in a 1-1 draw. McMillan had been left out of the starting line-up and replaced by George McLean, but he was reinstated for the replay. Celtic were poor and lost 3-0, with Jim Baxter emphasising his and Rangers superiority by sitting on the ball and inviting the Celtic players to come and get it! At the final whistle, Baxter grabbed the match ball and shoved it up his jersey, refusing to give it to referee Tiny Wharton. In the confines of the Rangers dressing-room, he handed it over to Man of the Match McMillan.

He played his last game for Rangers at St Johnstone in April 1964, after which the qualified quantity surveyor, who had always been a part-time player at Ibrox, went back to Airdrie.

He retired as a player in the summer of 1967 and then became coach, manager and subsequently a director of his home-town club. Though they may well have been his first and last love, there is no doubt that, in between, there had been golden Light Blue days. For his six years at Ibrox coincided with a period which brought as much concentrated success to the club as did any in its history.

## DAVE McPHERSON

**Born:** Paisley, 28 January 1964
**Rangers career:** 1981 to 1987
**Appearances and goals:**

| League | | FA Cup | | Lg Cup | | Europe | |
|---|---|---|---|---|---|---|---|
| A | G | A | G | A | G | A | G |
| 220/14 | 19 | 23 | 5 | 33/4 | 3 | 29 | 7 |

*Total appearances:* 305/18
*Total goals:* 34

**League Championships:** 1986-87; 1992-93; 1993-94
**Scottish Cup:** 1992-93;
**League Cup:** 1983-84; 1984-85; 1992-93; 1993-94
**Honours:** 27 Scotland caps

Though a series of high profile blunders put paid to Dave McPherson's Rangers career in what was his second spell with the club, he had proved himself an outstanding defender, as his medal collection shows.

He first broke into the Rangers league side as a teenager in 1982-83, and was immediately tipped as a great prospect for the future. Demonstrating his outstanding ability in the air, he looked set to be a fixture in the Light Blues defence for years to come. He made an impressive attacking gambit for the Ibrox club when he went forward for set pieces, and in one UEFA Cup tie against Valetta of Malta, scored four in an 8-0 win!

Even the arrival of Graeme Souness—the death knell for a number of players on Rangers' books at the time—failed to dislodge McPherson from the side. In Souness's first season in charge, he formed an impressive backbone to the club's defence with England international Terry Butcher as the side romped to their first League Championship in nine seasons, conceding a miserly 23 goals, including 11 League clean sheets in a row. Despite that winners' medal, a disaster in the Scottish Cup was to prove his undoing.

A home tie with Hamilton was widely expected to give the club an easy passage into the fourth round, but in one of the biggest upsets in the competition's history, a goal from Adrian Sprott in front of a disbelieving Ibrox sealed a humiliating 1-0 elimination. Souness blamed McPherson for the goal, and in the close season that followed he was dispatched to Hearts.

The determined defender showed his resolve. He became an inspiration for the perennially under-achieving Edinburgh side, and indeed won 24 of his 27 caps while with the Tynecastle club. His form proved so good that just prior to the European Championship finals in 1992, where he played for Scotland, Walter Smith re-signed him for Rangers in a £1.3 million deal.

There followed two seasons of honours, including an important role in the club's glorious European run of 1992-93 when Rangers came within a whisker of a place in the Champions Cup Final. McPherson was a top performer in the comprehensive Battle of Britain triumph over Leeds United. But despite a treble in his first campaign, by the tail end of the 1993-94 season, the fans were beginning to get on his back after some below-par performances. A catastrophic mix-up with Ally Maxwell, which allowed Dundee United's Craig Brewster to score the only goal of the Scottish Cup Final and deny Rangers a second consecutive treble, was a nail in his coffin.

When Rangers started the 1994-95 season poorly, he was made the scapegoat and parted company for a second time, again joining Hearts.

Though his departure was yet again under less than pleasing circumstances, it should not obscure the fact that Dave McPherson was a good player for Rangers over a long period of time.

He went on to score 37 goals in 416 games in his two spells with the Jam Tarts, before leaving the club in the summer of 1999 to take up the option of playing Australian football for Carlton.

## ALEXEI MIKHAILICHENKO

**Born:** Kiev, Ukraine, 30 March 1963
**Rangers career:** 1991 to 1995
**Appearances and goals:**

| League | | FA Cup | | Lg Cup | | Europe | |
|---|---|---|---|---|---|---|---|
| **A** | **G** | **A** | **G** | **A** | **G** | **A** | **G** |
| 74/36 | 20 | 9/3 | 3 | 5/5 | 2 | 5/1 | 0 |

*Total appearances:* 93/45
*Total goals:* 25
**League Championships:** 1991-92; 1992-93; 1993-94
**Scottish Cup:** 1991-92
**League Cup:** 1992-93
**Honours:** Soviet Union, CIS and Ukranian caps

Alexei Mikhailichenko became one of Walter Smith's first Ibrox recruits in 1991, and in just under five seasons with Rangers, won every domestic honour and a horde of new admirers. If there was regularly the impression that his work-rate and application was not all it could be, Mikhailitchenko's unquestionable flair earned him the forgiveness of many critics.

When Miko arrived in Scotland in the summer of 1991, from Sampdoria, expectation was high. He had come to the attention of Rangers while playing against the club for Dynamo Kiev in Europe a few years before, and indeed had been responsible for scoring the goal which gave the then Soviet champions a 1-0 win on their own turf.

One of Walter Smith's most imaginative signings, he also turned out to be one of the most infuriating! He let himself down on occasions with erratic displays and a tendency to wander in and out of games. On his day he was devastating, as was seen in a couple of Old Firm games and one superb Scottish Cup tie against Motherwell in the 1991-92 season. But there was also an unwillingness to impose himself on matches, with the result that he often became an anonymous and dispirited-looking figure on the pitch.

For someone who had played for Kiev—where he was voted Soviet Player of the Year in 1988 —and Serie 'A' Champions, Sampdoria, and captained the Commonwealth of Independent States in the European Championship Finals of 1992, he should have stood out in the SPL like a beacon, rather in the way that Brian Laudrup did. Sadly, there were no answers from the man himself, as he refused to conduct interviews in English, despite an apparent ability to speak the language well enough to make himself understood in the dressing room!

First and foremost a ball player, Mikhailichenko scored 10 goals in 24 starts in his first season at Ibrox as Rangers finished nine points ahead of runners-up Hearts. Far from being a flop, he helped Rangers to three successive titles in his first three seasons with the club, before injuries left him on the sidelines for much of the next two campaigns. It was widely felt that with his contract expiring in the summer of 1995 and a new visa required from the Department of Employment, Miko's number was up at Ibrox. However, goals in successive games against Hibernian and Kilmarnock were enough to earn him an extension to his contract.

The prospect of him teaming up in the middle of the park with Paul Gascoigne was an intriguing one, but it happened on only a handful of occasions before he left Rangers to return to Kiev. In probably the least significant match of his entire Ibrox career, the money-making testimonial for Scott Nisbet, he chose for some reason to put on an exhibition of ball skills which only served to underline that he was a very special player indeed!

After ending his playing career in 1997, a year after leaving Rangers, Mikhailichenko was appointed as assistant-manager to Dynamo Kiev manager Valeri Lobanovsky, and following Lobanovsky's untimely death at the age of 63, took charge of his country's most famous club.

## JIMMY MILLAR

**Born:** Edinburgh, 20 November 1934
**Rangers career:** 1955 to 1967
**Appearances and goals:**

| League | | FA Cup | | Lg Cup | | Europe | |
|---|---|---|---|---|---|---|---|
| **A** | **G** | **A** | **G** | **A** | **G** | **A** | **G** |
| 196/1 | 92 | 35 | 30 | 54 | 28 | 31 | 12 |

Total appearances: 316/1
Total goals: 162
**League Championships:** 1960-61; 1962-63; 1963-64
**Scottish Cup:** 1959-60; 1961-62; 1962-63; 1963-64
**League Cup:** 1960-61; 1961-62; 1964-65; 1965-66
**Honours:** 2 Scotland caps

Jimmy Millar was a half-back of outstanding promise when Rangers manager Scot Symon paid Dunfermline Athletic £5,000 for his services in January 1955. But after four years at the club, he was switched to centre-forward and became an overnight sensation!

In fact, in his first three seasons at Ibrox, Millar played in just three league games—all of them in different positions—before showing glimpses of what

*Jimmy Millar playing for Rangers during the 1965-66 season (www.snspix.com)*

was to come in 1957-58 when he played at both wing-half and inside-forward. Towards the end of the following season, Millar got his big break. Rangers were due to play Staevnet in a friendly in Denmark, but regular centre-forward Max Murray was injured. Millar replaced him and scored all his side's goals in a 4-0 win!

From then on, he proved himself a dashing centre-forward, as courageous as any player the Light Blues have ever had, and was the perfect foil for fellow strike partner Ralph Brand. They became known as the M and B Partnership, and Brand scored countless goals from chances created by Jimmy Millar.

In 1959-60, Millar scored 36 goals in all competitions, including 21 in the League. This total included a hat-trick against Clyde, followed a week later by all four goals at Arbroath. In that season's Scottish Cup he was outstanding, netting seven goals in seven games, including two headers in the final as Rangers beat Kilmarnock 2-0. The following season he won his first League Championship medal, playing in the opening 21 games before suffering a slipped disc in mid-January. Prior to that he had helped Rangers win the League Cup and had scored five goals in five European Cup Winners Cup ties. He had recovered from his back problem by the time Rangers met Borussia Moenchengladbach in the second leg of the final, but Rangers lost 2-1.

The following season he scored Rangers' opening goal in the League Cup Final replay win over Hearts, and was in superb form in that season's Scottish Cup competition, scoring seven goals in five games as Rangers reached the final. He scored four for the second time against Arbroath, and though he didn't find the net in the final, Rangers beat St Mirren 2-0.

Rangers won the League Championship again in 1962-63, thanks in the main to Millar having his best season in terms of goals scored, with 27 in 31 games. This total included another haul of four goals in the 5-0 hammering of Dundee United. Millar also netted hat-tricks against Sevilla in the European Cup Winners Cup, Dundee United in the Scottish Cup and two against Third Lanark in the League Cup. Millar's goal count that season was 43 in 50 games—his best-ever performance.

Millar played twice at full international level for Scotland, scoring twice on his debut in the infamous match against Austria. The referee abandoned the game with Scotland leading 4-1, after Austria lost their heads and had two of their players sent off.

In the glorious treble-winning season of 1963-64, Millar spent most of the season on the treatment table, but was in the side for the Scottish Cup Final against Dundee when he scored twice in a 3-1 win. He won a further League Cup winners' medal the following season as Celtic were beaten 2-1, and completed his haul with a another in the same competition against the same opposition in 1966 when he played at wing-half.

In the summer of 1967 he joined Dundee United and later had a spell as manager of Raith Rovers.

# ALEX MILLER

**Born:** Glasgow, 7 April 1949
**Rangers career:** 1967 to 1983
**Appearances and goals:**

| League | | FA Cup | | Lg Cup | | Europe | |
|---|---|---|---|---|---|---|---|
| **A** | **G** | **A** | **G** | **A** | **G** | **A** | **G** |
| 159/38 | 17 | 18/9 | 1 | 53/10 | 12 | 15/4 | 0 |

*Total appearances:* 245/61

*Total goals:* 30

**League Championships:** 1974-75; 1975-76; 1977-78
**Scottish Cup:** 1975-76; 1978-79
**League Cup:** 1970-71; 1977-78; 1978-79; 1981-82

One of the club's most versatile players, Alex Miller arrived at Ibrox in the summer of 1967 having played his early football for Clydebank Juniors. Initially he was a centre-forward and scored goals galore in Rangers' reserve side.

Though he made his debut as a substitute for centre-half Ronnie McKinnon in the penultimate game of the 1968-69 season, a 1-1 home draw against Dundee, many of his best performances came after he had been switched to left-back. He didn't appear at all the following season, but then in 1970-71 he appeared on a much more regular basis. In fact, he lined up in the Rangers side for that season's League Cup Final against Celtic, a match the Gers won 1-0. In fact, he played the entire ninety minutes despite suffering from a broken jaw sustained during the early stages of the game.

Injuries then hampered his progress, and he found himself in and out of the side for the next few seasons, though by the mid-seventies he was playing well enough to keep Scottish international Sandy Jardine out of the Rangers team.

Though he went on to appear for the club in virtually every outfield position, Alex Miller probably suffered for his great versatility. He was the ideal substitute—not only able to fill in any position but a player who was always able to produce a thoroughly reliable game. Tall and slim, Miller wasn't the most skilled player ever to pull on a Rangers shirt, but he was certainly one of the most dedicated to the Rangers cause.

Though he scored very few goals, he was deadly from the penalty-spot and became the club's most successful penalty-taker since the days of Johnny Hubbard. Very few goalkeepers had moved before the ball lay nestled in the net behind them!

Miller won his first League Championship medal in 1975-76 as Rangers completed the treble, but he missed the League Cup Final win over Celtic after having scored four goals from the spot in the competition's previous nine games. He was to make amends though by winning three further League Cup winners' medals during his time at Ibrox.

Alex Miller went on to give the club great service and was hugely popular with the Rangers faithful, appearing in over 300 games before being released by Rangers manager John Greig. He then quickly built a successful management career with, in turn, Morton, St Mirren and finally Hibernian.

## MICHAEL MOLS

**Born:** Amsterdam, Holland, 17 December 1970
**Rangers career:** 1999 to 2004
**Appearances and goals:**

| League | | FA Cup | | Lg Cup | | Europe | |
|---|---|---|---|---|---|---|---|
| **A** | **G** | **A** | **G** | **A** | **G** | **A** | **G** |
| 79/20 | 38 | 7/2 | 1 | 5/4 | 2 | 22/8 | 7 |

*Total appearances:* 113/34
*Total goals:* 48
**League Championships:** 2002-03
**Scottish Cup:** 2002-03
**League Cup:** 2002-03
**Honours:** 6 Holland caps

Michael Mols' time at Ibrox was blighted by a knee injury sustained in a 1999 Champions League encounter with Bayern Munich, although he did recover to help Rangers win the Treble in 2002-03.

Mols was a product of Ajax's famous youth system of the early 1990s, but made his professional debut with Cambuur Leeuwarden in 1992. A stint with FC Twente followed before a move to FC Utrecht, where he became a club icon and broke into the Dutch national side, going on to make six appearances for the Oranje.

Mols signed for Rangers, then managed by Dick Advocaat, in the summer of 1999. Because of the low status of Scottish football in Europe, Rangers were again forced to play two qualifying rounds in the European Cup in season 1999-2000. Mols, in his first game for the club, scored twice in their second round 4-1 defeat away of Finland's FC Haka and helped to make another of the goals.

He missed the club's opening league game, but scored on his debut in a 4-0 win at Hearts. Then on his home league debut against Motherwell, Mols scored all his side's goals in a 4-0 defeat of the Steelmen. He also scored two in his next game at Ibrox as Aberdeen were beaten 3-1, and had scored nine goals in nine league games when injury struck in a Champions League game against Bayern Munich. Mols, who had scored two goals in a 4-1 win over PSV Eindhoven, saw his season ended when he suffered serious cruciate ligament damage after a clash with keeper Oliver Kahn.

The tricky Dutchman, who was extremely popular with Rangers fans, had to undergo three operations in the months following that fateful night in November 1999, and didn't return to the team until ten months later against Dundee. However, he continued to suffer fitness problems over the next couple of seasons, and was in and out of the Rangers side, although when he did make an appearance, he was always dangerous.

However, in 2002-03, Mols was back to his best, helping the club complete the Treble. He scored 13 goals in 23 starts in the SPL, including doubles in four of those games, and netted one of the goals in the 4-3 Scottish Cup semi-final win over Motherwell before playing in the 1-0 final win over Dundee. He had already picked up a League Cup winners' medal after Rangers had beaten Celtic 2-1 earlier in the campaign.

In 2004, Mols returned to his homeland, signing on for another—this time unsuccessful—stint at FC Utrecht before switching to ADO Den Haag a year later. But following the club's ultimately successful fight against relegation, he opted to call time on his playing career.

## CRAIG MOORE

**Born:** Canterbury, Australia, 12 December 1975
**Rangers career:** 1993 to 1998 and 1999 to 2005
**Appearances and goals:**

| League | | FA Cup | | Lg Cup | | Europe | |
|---|---|---|---|---|---|---|---|
| **A** | **G** | **A** | **G** | **A** | **G** | **A** | **G** |
| 170/5 | 14 | 20 | 2 | 15/1 | 0 | 42 | 1 |

*Total appearances:* 247/6
*Total goals:* 17
**League Championships:** 1994-95; 1996-97; 1999-2000; 2002-03
**Scottish Cup:** 1999-2000; 2001-02; 2002-03
**League Cup:** 1996-97; 2002-03
**Honours:** 37 Australia caps

Craig Moore's arrival at Ibrox is a fairy tale! As a boy in Australia, he wrote to top British clubs asking for trials. Paying his own way over, he attempted to make the grade at both Arsenal and Rangers. He instantly impressed in Glasgow, whereas at Highbury, he felt more ill-at-ease. In fact, the young Australian believed some of the big names at the Gunners felt he was a threat to them, and so he needed little persuasion when a contract from the Light Blues was on offer.

With Gary Stevens' career at the club drawing to a close and young blood required, Moore made his debut against Dundee United in April 1994, and then at the start of the following campaign began to establish himself. While in years gone by, other youngsters at the club had been offered openings, few took advantage of them to the extent that Craig Moore did.

Having helped Rangers win the League Championship in 1994-95 when

*Craig Moore's header is cleared off the goal line as Rangers meet Manchester United in the 2003 Champions League (www.snspix.com)*

he scored the club's final goal of the campaign in a 1-1 home draw with Partick Thistle, he collected a second Championship medal two seasons later, when he also helped Rangers win the League Cup, beating Hearts 4-3 in the final.

During the early stages of the 1998-99 season, Moore opted for a move to Terry Venables' Crystal Palace side, where he immediately impressed with his strength and tackling, allied to his aerial ability. He also netted three times in his first five games for the Eagles, but he was forced to return to Ibrox towards the end of the campaign when the transfer fee was not forthcoming.

In 1999-2000 Moore collected his third League Championship winners' medal as Rangers finished 21 points ahead of runners-up Celtic, and won his first Scottish Cup medal after Aberdeen had been beaten 4-0. Injuries disrupted his next campaign, but he was back to pick up another Scottish Cup winners' medal in 2001-02, with arch-rivals Celtic being on the wrong end in a five-goal thriller. Moore missed very few games the following season as Rangers completed the Treble, and remained an important member of the Rangers' defence until the beginning of the 2004-05 season.

Moore was the captain of the 'Olyroos', the Australian Olympic football team at the 2004 Olympics at Athens, when they managed to reached the quarter-finals. However, his involvement angered Rangers manager Alex McLeish, as it forced him to miss the start of the Scottish League season. As a result, Moore was stripped of the club captaincy and was forced to the fringes of the team. In January 2005 he was sold to Borussia Moenchengladbach, where he teamed up with former Rangers manager Dick Advocaat.

However, Advocaat was sacked after a short time in charge, and Moore left the German club after a falling out with club management. He joined Newcastle United and made his competitive debut in an FA Cup quarter-final against Chelsea, after which he was an ever-present, helping the Magpies win an Inter Toto Cup place. His form led to him representing Australia in the 2006 World Cup Finals, where he scored a penalty against Croatia, enabling Australia to progress to the second round.

In May 2007, it was announced that his contract would not be renewed, and he returned to Australia to play for Queensland Rovers. His career there did not start well, as he was sent off on his debut!

## MAX MURRAY

**Born:** Falkirk, 7 November 1935
**Rangers career:** 1955 to 1963
**Appearances and goals:**

| League | | FA Cup | | Lg Cup | | Europe | |
|---|---|---|---|---|---|---|---|
| A | G | A | G | A | G | A | G |
| 103 | 80 | 16 | 19 | 27 | 19 | 8 | 3 |

*Total appearances:* 154
*Total goals:* 121
**League Championships:** 1956-57; 1958-59

Affectionately known as 'Slapsie Maxie', Murray arrived at Ibrox from Queen's Park in the summer of 1955 with a reputation for being a prolific goalscorer.

Having scored on his debut for Rangers in a 5-0 League Cup win at his home-town club Falkirk, he failed to get on the scoresheet in his first League game as Rangers played out a goalless home draw against Stirling Albion. Despite finding himself an understudy to Kitchenbrand, Baird and Simpson, he still managed to score nine goals in the 13 League and Cup games in which he appeared.

In 1956-57, Murray was the club's top scorer with 29 goals in 30 league games as Rangers pipped Hearts to the title. Though failing to net a hat-trick, he did score in eight consecutive games midway through the campaign. Prior to this he had netted a double in the 5-3 home win over the Jam Tarts, the club's nearest rivals.

Murray continued to find the net on a regular basis the following season, and though Hearts ran away with the Championship, Murray managed to score hat-tricks in all competitions. His first treble came on the opening day of the season as St Mirren were beaten 6-0 in a League Cup tie, followed by three in the 5-0 League victory over Aberdeen. Murray's third and final hat-trick of that season came in the Scottish Cup as Rangers thrashed Forfar Athletic 9-1 on their own ground.

Murray won a second League Championship medal in 1958-59, when his 17 goals in 22 games included another hat-trick as runners-up Hearts were demolished 5-0 in front of a 66,000 crowd at Ibrox.

Surprisingly, after this, he found himself playing mainly in the club's reserves, his place having been taken by Jimmy Millar. Yet whenever he was called upon, he never let the team down. An all-action player, he had just one thought in mind and that was to direct the ball toward goal, whether it be with his right foot, left foot or his head! Yet he was always the most popular of players with Rangers fans. There were numerous occasions when he would slash wildly at balls and blast them over the bar when often a simple side foot would have been more effective!

Yet even so, he did score some vital goals for the club. Recalled to the side in place of the injured Millar in the 1961-62 Scottish Cup semi-final, he scored twice in a 3-1 win over Motherwell, yet lost out to Millar when the side to face St Mirren in the final was selected.

In November 1962 Murray was transferred to West Bromwich Albion, but couldn't settle at the Hawthorns and returned north of the border to continue his career with Third Lanark. Murray was also a capable golfer, playing to a two handicap.


## GEORGE NIVEN

**Born:** Blairhall, date not found
**Rangers career:** 1951 to 1961
**Appearances and goals:**

| League | | FA Cup | | Lg Cup | | Europe | |
|---|---|---|---|---|---|---|---|
| **A** | **G** | **A** | **G** | **A** | **G** | **A** | **G** |
| 221 | 0 | 32 | 0 | 59 | 0 | 15 | 0 |

*Total appearances:* 327
*Total goals:* 0
**League Championships:** 1952-53; 1955-56; 1956-57; 1958-59; 1960-61
**Scottish Cup:** 1952-53; 1959-60
**League Cup:** 1960-61

Though he was on the small side for a goalkeeper, George Niven was a thoroughly reliable keeper over a good number of seasons at Ibrox, after making his debut on the final day of the 1951-52 season in a 1-1 draw against Aberdeen at Pittodrie.

In the opening game of the following season, Bobby Brown was in goal as Rangers were trounced 5-0 by Hearts in the League Cup. It was Brown's last game for the Light Blues, as he was replaced by the courageous Niven. Niven then became the club's first-choice keeper throughout the 1950s, until losing his place at the start of the next decade to Billy Ritchie.

In his first full season, Niven helped Rangers win the League Championship on goal difference from Hibernian, and was between the posts when the Gers played Aberdeen in the Scottish Cup Final. In the 27th minute, he suffered a head injury in going down at the feet of the Dons' Paddy Buckley, and had to be helped off with blood streaming from the wound. George Young took his place in goal, but a brave Niven appeared for the second half with his head swathed in bandages after receiving four stitches. Despite Aberdeen equalising Rangers' earlier goal, Niven was outstanding as the game went to a replay. In the second game, Niven wore a leather helmet and kept a clean sheet as Billy Simpson scored the game's only goal.

Of course he also had his bad games and without doubt the worst of them was the 1957 League Cup Final when Celtic thrashed Rangers 7-1. This of course prompted the rather unsubtle Celtic joke, 'What's the time? Seven past Niven.'

Though he picked up further League Championship medals in 1955-56, 1956-57 and 1958-59, probably his best season was 1959-60 when he was in outstanding form throughout the campaign, and was selected to play for Scotland against England. Unfortunately, injury in the Scottish Cup semi-final against rivals Celtic caused him to withdraw. It proved to be his only Scottish selection. Billy Ritchie played in the semi-final replay which Rangers won 4-1, but Niven was back between the posts for the final when Rangers defeated Kilmarnock 2-0.

The following season proved to be Niven's last at Ibrox, as he won his fifth League Championship medal and picked up his first League Cup winners' medal as Rangers defeated Kilmarnock again 2-0. The Rugby Park club had been runners-up to the Gers in the League and had beaten Rangers in both of that season's encounters.

Having played the last of his 327 matches against Motherwell in March 1961, Niven moved on to play for Partick Thistle in February of the following year. There he continued to play on with distinction in what was one of the Jag's best-ever teams.

## NACHO NOVO

**Born:** Ferrol, Galicia, Spain, 26 March 1979
**Rangers career:** 2004 to Present

**Appearances and goals:**

| League | | FA Cup | | Lg Cup | | Europe | |
|---|---|---|---|---|---|---|---|
| **A** | **G** | **A** | **G** | **A** | **G** | **A** | **G** |
| 67/25 | 27 | 3/1 | 0 | 6/1 | 3 | 15/5 | 7 |

Total appearances: 91/32
Total goals: 37
**League Championships:** 2004-05
**League Cup:** 2004-05

Nacho Novo ended lots of speculation about his future when he finally signed for Rangers in the summer of 2004—becoming Alex McLeish's sixth summer signing.

Born in Northern Spain, he began his career with SD Huesca before joining Raith Rovers in July 2001. He was an instant hit at Stark's Park, scoring 20 goals in 37 appearances, and it wasn't too long before he attracted the attention of Premier League Dundee. Novo signed for the Dark Blues for a nominal fee in the summer of 2002.

He remained at Dundee for two seasons, netting 25 goals in his second campaign at Dens Park as well as helping the club reach the first round of the UEFA Cup. His form attracted the interest of several clubs. Both Rangers and Celtic as well as Leicester City were reported to be interested in signing Novo, however the Hoops dropped their interest in the player and Leicester City's offer failed to materialise.

He eventually signed for Rangers in July 2004 for a reported fee of £450,000 and, wearing the No.10 shirt, made his debut on the opening day of the 2004-05 season as Rangers played out a goalless draw at Aberdeen. He went on to have a wonderful first season, scoring 25 goals in 48 games in all competitions. This included 19 in the League as Rangers pipped Celtic for the title, Novo's last goal proving the crucial winner on the final day against Hibernian. He also scored in the 5-1 League Cup Final triumph over Motherwell, and netted one against eventual UEFA Cup winners CSKA Moscow in the qualifying stages of the Champions League. This was the club's first-ever loss to a club from either Russia or the former Soviet Union.

However, controversy was never too far away. In November 2004, a death threat was painted near his house, while in the previous month he had his car tyres slashed!

On the pitch he received a red card in the SPL match at Hibernian—although it was later reduced to a yellow—while he was subject to an SPL inquiry, which was launched after he appeared to kick out at Celtic's Jackie McNamara and Stephen Pearson in a fiery Old Firm derby in November. Novo received a one-match ban and 12 additional disciplinary points for his actions.

Despite this controversy his accomplishments were rewarded with a nomination for the players' Player of the Year, although he eventually lost out to joint-winners John Hartson and team-mate Fernando Ricksen.

Novo was a regular in the Rangers side until the early stages of the 2005-06 season when he broke his fifth metatarsal, ruling him out for several months. He made his first Rangers comeback against Kilmarnock in a 3-2 win, but failed to show any level of consistency for the remainder of the campaign and was left frustrated with limited appearances in the first team.

After limited first team opportunities under new manager Paul Le Guen, Novo looked set for a move to Coventry City, but the proposed transfer fell through on transfer deadline day. He remained at Ibrox and scored his first goal in over a year in a 3-2 UEFA Cup win over AS Livorno Calcio in October 2006. He then came off the bench to score a late winner against St Mirren, and after starting against Motherwell was named Man of the Match. His rejuvenated form continued with goals against Hearts, Maccabi Haifa and Auxerre, and after stating his desire to play for the Gers for the rest of his career, his natural goalscoring ability could yet prove decisive in the forthcoming season's SPL campaign.

## ARTHUR NUMAN

**Born:** Heemskerk, Holland, 14 December 1969
**Rangers career:** 1998 to 2003
**Appearances and goals:**

| League | | FA Cup | | Lg Cup | | Europe | |
|---|---|---|---|---|---|---|---|
| **A** | **G** | **A** | **G** | **A** | **G** | **A** | **G** |
| 113/5 | 3 | 13 | 2 | 12/1 | 1 | 31 | 0 |

Total appearances: 169/6
Total goals: 6
**League Championships:** 1999-2000; 2002-03
**Scottish Cup:** 1999-2000; 2001-02; 2002-03
**League Cup:** 2001-02
**Honours:** 45 Holland caps

Dutch international left-back Arthur Numan arrived at Ibrox from PSV Eindhoven in May 1998 for a Scottish then record fee of £5 million.

He started his career with Dutch amateur club SV Beverwijk, and was quickly spotted by Haarlem. He originally played in a more attacking role as opposed to the playing style of his later career, although his long-time mentor Dick Advocaat, then the coach of Haarlem, decided to field him at left-back—a move which quickly saw him rise to recognition within the Eredivisie.

In the summer of 1991, Numan joined FC Twente where he was appointed captain and skippered the Dutch Under-21 team. However, it was not until he joined PSV Eindhoven that his talents were fully appreciated, and with

Advocaat now the national team manager he was given his full international debut against Poland.

More domestic success was to follow in a big club such as PSV, and he was selected to represent the Dutch team in the 1994 World Cup Finals. Injuries forced him to miss Euro '96, but he was back in the side for the 1998 World Cup in France. A second yellow card against Argentina forced him to miss the crucial semi-final clash with Brazil, though he was back for the third place match against Croatia.

At the end of the tournament, Numan joined Rangers, although his first season at Ibrox was blighted by recurring injuries. Manager Dick Advocaat waited patiently for the left-back to recover, and his patience was rewarded the following season as Rangers won the League title and the Scottish Cup, beating Aberdeen 4-0 in the final. Numan was awarded the team's vice-captaincy, serving as deputy to Lorenzo Amoruso. He also teamed up with a team of very talented individuals, including Michael Mols, Ronald de Boer and Fernando Ricksen. In particular, he had a prolific relationship with German international left-sided midfielder Jorg Albertz.

In 2002-03, Numan helped Rangers win the Treble, although he was missing from the League Cup Final side that defeated Celtic. Towards the end of that campaign, he informed the club that he could not agree a deal with them and that he would mutually terminate the contract come the close season. He stated that he was willing to accept a pay-cut offer, but felt that Rangers had underrated him.

Numan then announced his retirement, with a late offer from Villareal of the Spanish La Liga failing to convince him carry on playing. He refused to continue his career in Holland, as he was not looking forward to starting training again and playing hectic games every week.

He can now be seen as a regular pundit on Scotsport SPL, Scottish and Grampian TV's round-up of Scottish Premier League action.

## DEREK PARLANE

**Born:** Helensburgh, 5 May 1953
**Rangers career:** 1970 to 1980
**Appearances and goals:**

| League | | FA Cup | | Lg Cup | | Europe | |
|---|---|---|---|---|---|---|---|
| A | G | A | G | A | G | A | G |
| 168/34 | 80 | 20/5 | 8 | 44/7 | 21 | 19/3 | 2 |

Total appearances: 251/49
Total goals: 111
**League Championships:** 1974-75; 1975-76; 1977-78
**Scottish Cup:** 1972-73; 1978-79
**League Cup:** 1975-76; 1977-78; 1978-79
**Honours:** 12 Scotland caps

*In the 1973 Scottish Cup semi-final against Ayr, Derek Parlane breaks past goalkeeper Dave Stewart (www.snspix.com)*

Son of the former Rangers inside-forward Jimmy Parlane, Derek was a midfield player converted into a centre-forward by the Light Blues' boss Jock Wallace.

Willie Thornton and Willie Waddell together had gone down to the village of Rhu on the Clyde estuary to sign the young Parlane as a teenager, against very strong competition from a number of other clubs, when he was a Queen's Park player.

Having made his Rangers debut in a 3-1 defeat at Falkirk on New Year's Day 1971, Parlane later impressed himself on a much wider audience in the European Cup Winners' Cup semi-final of 1971-72 against Bayern Munich, when he replaced the injured John Greig at right-half. The youngster had the game of his life, volleying home a Willie Johnston corner-kick in a 2-0 second leg win which took the club through to the final.

The following season saw him net Rangers first goal in a 3-2 Scottish Cup Final victory over Celtic, while in 1973-74 he scored 22 goals in 39 games, including a League Cup hat-trick against Dumbarton and a Scottish Cup treble against his former club Queen's Park. In the League encounter with Hearts on 19 January 1974, Parlane scored all four goals in a 4-0 defeat of the Jam Tarts. In doing so, he scored Rangers' 6000th League goal.

In 1974-75, Parlane won his first League Championship medal, his total of 17 goals including five goals in a 6-1 win at Dunfermline Athletic and a hat-trick in a 3-3 home draw with Kilmarnock. Tall, strong and energetic, his form had seen him win full international honours, and despite being a contemporary of Derek Johnstone, he was Rangers' leading scorer in four seasons out of five.

He continued to win a clutch of domestic honours while at Ibrox, but in March 1980, he parted company with the club, signing for Leeds United. Although he scored on his debut for the Yorkshire club, goals did not come easy and he later spent a period on loan to Hong Kong club Bulova.

It was only when he joined Manchester City in the summer of 1983 that he recaptured his scoring form. In January 1985 he began a four-month loan spell with Swansea City before trying his luck with Racing Jet of Belgium. On his return to the British Isles, he joined Rochdale, but a financial crisis at Spotland saw manager Eddie Gray release him. He joined another old Leeds boy and fellow Scottish international Gordon McQueen at Airdrie, before playing non-League football for Macclesfield Town, for whom he later became a director.

## CRAIG PATERSON

**Born:** South Queensferry, 2 October 1959
**Rangers career:** 1982 to 1987
**Appearances and goals:**

| League | | FA Cup | | Lg Cup | | Europe | |
|---|---|---|---|---|---|---|---|
| A | G | A | G | A | G | A | G |
| 83 | 4 | 8 | 0 | 26 | 5 | 13 | 3 |

*Total appearances:* 130
*Total goals:* 12
**League Cup:** 1983-84; 1984-85

The son of John Paterson, a centre-half in the Hibernian team of the late fifties and early sixties, it was perhaps fitting that his career should also begin at Easter Road, where he had shown immense promise and ability.

His displays for the Edinburgh club attracted the attention of a number of leading clubs north and south of the border, and Rangers were so desperate to have him in their ranks that they signed him prior to a pre-season tournament in Lille, and they did not insist on a medical examination before the transfer fee of £225,000 was paid! Paterson made his Rangers debut in the tournament and scored the winning goal in the semi-final against favourites St Etienne in a penalty shoot-out. They then unfortunately lost the final to SK Lokeren.

Sadly, injuries dogged his time at Ibrox, although he was a regular first teamer in his first four seasons at the club. He soon established himself at the heart of the Rangers team, forming a successful central defensive partnership with Northern Ireland international John McClelland. When McClelland parted company with the club, Paterson was appointed captain and led the team to success in the 1984-85 League Cup Final against Dundee United—a match Rangers won 1-0.

It was his second successive League Cup winners' medal, for the previous season he had been a member of the Rangers team that beat Celtic 3-2 in the final, courtesy of an Ally McCoist hat-trick.

There is little doubt that Craig Paterson's greatest strength was in the air, and he was a ball-player rather than just a plain stopper. Towards the end of his stay at Ibrox, injuries and intermittent lapses in form prevented him from being the great player he should have been, and fulfilling all his talents. Such was Paterson's ability that he should most certainly have won full international honours for Scotland, although he did play at Under-21 level.

During the early stages of Graeme Souness's regime, Paterson was transferred to Motherwell for a fee of £20,000. A sound reader of the game, he gave Tommy McLean's side a very necessary solidity at the back and his partnership with Tom McAdam was a defensive cornerstone at Fir Park. A Scottish Cup winner with the Steelmen, he eventually fell foul of Tommy McLean and was sold to Kilmarnock for £50,000 in October 1991.

Paterson thrived at Rugby Park, helping Killie win promotion to the SPL as champions of the First Division in 1992-93.

## ANDY PENMAN

**Born:** Rosyth, 20 February 1943
**Rangers career:** 1967 to 1973
**Appearances and goals:**

| League | | FA Cup | | Lg Cup | | Europe | |
|---|---|---|---|---|---|---|---|
| A | G | A | G | A | G | A | G |
| 88/13 | 36 | 12 | 4 | 16/3 | 7 | 17/1 | 2 |

*Total appearances:* 133/17
*Total goals:* 49
**Honours:** 3 Scotland caps

A midfield player of class and startling vision, Andy Penman had been something of a boy prodigy. After representing Dunfermline Schools, he had gone to Everton, making his debut there in a Lancashire Senior Cup match against Liverpool at the age of just fifteen. Returning to Scotland, he joined Dundee and made his debut for them when not quite sixteen and still an amateur.

Penman was capped for Scotland at schoolboy, youth, amateur, Under-23 and senior level, and while with Dundee won a League Championship medal in 1961-62. Also he played for the Dark Blues in the 1964 Scottish Cup Final against Rangers, with the Light Blues running out 3-1 winners.

He arrived at Ibrox in April 1967 in exchange for George McLean and

£30,000, and though he surprisingly won nothing at all on the domestic front, he did add a couple of full international caps to his collection. Penman was a fine passer of the ball who could clip balls precisely through, round or over opposition defences to give the Rangers forwards clear runs on goal.

This was probably never better demonstrated than in the 1971 Scottish Cup Final against arch-rivals Celtic. Time and time again, he carved out openings for the likes of Colin Stein and Willie Johnston, but each time they failed to capitalise on them. The first meeting was drawn 1-1, but even though Penman repeated his performance in the replay, the chances again went begging and Celtic won 2-1.

Fitness and health were great problems for Andy Penman, and as a diabetic, he was prone to putting on weight.

Though he was more of a creator of goals than a goalscorer, he did average a goal every three games in all competitions, with a best return of 15 in 26 starts during the 1968-69 season when Rangers were runners-up to Celtic. Rangers were to finish runners-up to their greatest rivals in each of Penman's first three seasons with the club. He also reached double figures in terms of league goals in 1969-70, when one of his best performances came as he netted twice in a 3-2 defeat of fellow title challengers Hearts towards the end of the campaign.

Penman used dead-ball situations to telling effect, either bringing his team-mates into the action with pin-point accuracy or forcing outstanding saves from the opposition keepers. With a little more luck, he could well have been one of the historically memorable Rangers players.

On parting company with the Gers, Penman joined Arbroath before moving on to Inverness Caledonian where he ended his career in 1979.

## JOHN PRENTICE

**Born:** Shotts, 1926.
**Died:** Australia, 10 February 2006
**Rangers career:** 1950 to 1956
**Appearances and goals:**

| League | | FA Cup | | Lg Cup | | Europe | |
|---|---|---|---|---|---|---|---|
| A | G | A | G | A | G | A | G |
| 96 | 18 | 16 | 8 | 30 | 11 | - | - |

**League Championships:** 1952-53;
**Scottish Cup:** 1952-53

John Prentice was strong and powerful, and worked the ball well, particularly with his left foot. He played with equal skill whether he turned out at left-half or inside-left, where he formed a potent wing partnership with Johnny Hubbard.

Prentice arrived at Ibrox from Heart of Midlothian in March 1950, with

Rangers paying £7,000 for his services. He made his Rangers debut in a surprise 2-1 defeat at Airdrie towards the end of the 1950-51 season—a campaign in which the Light Blues finished runners-up to Hibernian, and Airdrie just avoided the drop by a single point!

He appeared in the majority of Rangers games in 1951-52 as they once again challenged Hibernian for the League title, but again had to be satisfied with the runners-up spot. During the course of the campaign, Prentice scored his first goal for the club in a 5-1 win at Stirling Albion. It was a different story the following season, as Rangers won both the League Championship and the Scottish Cup. Prentice was an ever-present, scoring eight goals in his 30 appearances and appearing in the first match of the Scottish Cup Final against Aberdeen and scoring Rangers' goal in a 1-1 draw. An injury kept him out of the replay which the Gers won 1-0, thanks to a Billy Simpson goal.

Though not a prolific scorer, Prentice did find the net on a regular basis in the League Cup competition, and in 1953-54 netted a hat-trick in a 4-2 quarter-final first leg defeat of Ayr United.

He continued to be a regular in the Rangers side over the next couple of seasons but by the time Rangers again won the League Championship, Prentice found himself on the fringes of the team and didn't qualify for a medal as he only made ten appearances in that 1955-56 season.

In September 1956, Prentice left Rangers for £2,500 to play for Falkirk, and during his time with the club captained the Bairns to a Scottish Cup victory over Kilmarnock.

At the end of his playing days, Prentice became a coach and later had a successful spell as manager with Clyde. Former Dundee United manager Jim McLean, one of the longest-serving in the game, once claimed that John Prentice was the biggest influence on his career—saying that everything he knew about coaching he learned from Prentice.

In the 1960s, Prentice was appointed Scotland's team manager, albeit for a few months. Even before his terms had been agreed, he went to Canada for a job interview without mentioning this to the Scottish FA selection committee. Not surprisingly they thought this was less than discreet, and he was invited to move on! He later emigrated to Australia where he died of a brain tumour in 2006.

## DAVIE PROVAN

**Born:** Falkirk, 11 March 1941
**Rangers career:** 1958 to 1970
**Appearances and goals:**

| League | | FA Cup | | Lg Cup | | Europe | |
|---|---|---|---|---|---|---|---|
| A | G | A | G | A | G | A | G |
| 170 | 9 | 20 | 1 | 50 | 1 | 21/1 | 0 |

Total appearances: 261/1
Total goals: 11
**League Championships:** 1963-64
**Scottish Cup:** 1962-63; 1963-64; 1965-66
**League Cup:** 1963-64; 1964-65
**Honours:** 5 Scotland caps

Davie Provan's Rangers career was launched and ended as a result of a broken leg!

He arrived at Ibrox from Bonnyvale Star as a centre-half, but was kept out of the first team by the likes of McKinnon and Paterson. However, he was also able to play in either full-back position, and when Eric Caldow had the misfortune to break his leg in the Wembley international of 1963, Provan took his chance.

He was a member of the Rangers side that won the Treble in 1963-64, and having developed from a solid club craftsman into an international class defender, he made his Scotland debut in October of that season against Northern Ireland. He went on to win five full caps, having already represented the country at Under-23 level and played for the Scottish League XI.

During his time with Rangers, Davie Provan established full-back partnerships with Caldow, Bobby Shearer and Kai Johansen, and won further honours in both Cup competitions. He also played for Rangers in the 1967 European Cup Winners Cup Final when the Light Blues lost 1-0 to Bayern Munich.

A player of some repute, his Rangers career was effectively ended when a rather crude challenge from Celtic's Bertie Auld in the first Old Firm game of the 1967-68 season badly broke Provan's leg. Though he tried to make a comeback, he was never quite the same player again, and after managing just 17 further league appearances, he was released by Rangers boss Willie Waddell.

Provan moved into English football with Crystal Palace, but made just one appearance for the Eagles before switching to Plymouth Argyle.

He stayed at Home Park for four seasons, appearing in 128 games for the Pilgrims before returning to Scotland to see out his career with St Mirren. On hanging up his boots, Provan

*Davie Provan (www.snspix.com)*

remained at Love Street as assistant-manager to Alex Ferguson. He later had a spell as manager of Albion Rovers before working as chief scout for Rangers under the management of John Greig.

After ending his involvement with the game, Provan and Bertie Auld became great golfing buddies, proving that time is in fact a great healer!

## DADO PRSO

**Born:** Zadar, Croatia, 5 November 1974
**Rangers career:** 2004 to 2007
**Appearances and goals:**

| League | | FA Cup | | Lg Cup | | Europe | |
|---|---|---|---|---|---|---|---|
| A | G | A | G | A | G | A | G |
| 85/9 | 31 | 1/1 | 0 | 3/2 | 2 | 17/5 | 4 |

*Total appearances:* 106/17
*Total goals:* 37
**League Championships:** 2004-05
**League Cup:** 2004-05
**Honours:** 32 Croatia caps

A former car mechanic, Croatian international striker Dado Prso really rose to prominence just before he signed for Rangers, having commanded the attention of Europe when his goals fired AS Monaco to the Champions League Final in May 2004.

Prso started out with his hometown club NK Zadar, and was briefly with Hajduk Split before signing for NK Pazinka. Failing to make much impact with any of these clubs, he moved to France to play for FC Rouen and then Fourth Division San Raphael. It was whilst playing in a friendly against Monaco that he came to the attention of their manager, Jean Tigana.

Initially he played second team football alongside the likes of Thierry Henry and David Trezeguet, before joining Corsican club Ajaccio on loan. He spent a couple of seasons with the French Second Division side, scoring 21 goals in 53 appearances. He returned to Monaco in 1999 and helped them win the French title that season—it was Prso's goal against Caen which sealed their last title triumph.

Prso also helped AS Monaco to the UEFA Champions League Final in 2004, and is well remembered for his four-goal performance in the 8-3 drubbing of Deportivo de La Coruna—a game played on his birthday—the highest scoring match in Champions League history.

His form for the French side earned him a call-up to the Croatian national team. He scored on his debut and helped them secure a place in Euro 2004. He is best remembered in this tournament for the one goal he scored against France in Leiria. Over time he became an essential part of the Croatian attack formation and contributed greatly to his side's successes.

*An audacious overhead kick by Dado Prso in a 2007 game against Motherwell*
*(www.snspix.com)*

Prso joined Rangers in the summer of 2004, and his first season for the Gers proved a great success as he made 46 appearances in all competitions and scored 21 goals. Eighteen of these came in the League as Rangers won the Championship by a point from Celtic and lifted the League Cup. Prso had netted in the quarter-final victory over Celtic and in the 7-1 semi-final drubbing of Dundee United. Perhaps his one black mark in the season came in March, when he was sent off in the game against Hearts.

At Ibrox, Prso exhibited a somewhat peculiar problem with his knees—after every game where he lasts the ninety minutes, they get swollen to the extent that he sometimes cannot play for several days, and this reduced his appearances in 2005-06. Even so, departing Rangers manager Alex McLeish described Prso as his 'best Rangers signing'.

He remained a member of the 2006-07 Rangers team under new boss Paul Le Guen and then his replacement Walter Smith. After announcing his retirement from international football, it was announced he would be leaving Rangers when his contract expired in the summer of 2007 due to his recurring knee problems. At his last game at Ibrox he walked out wearing a brace on his leg due to damage to his ankle. He was then given a 'Guard of Honour' by his team-mates, before going back up the tunnel with tears in his eyes.

## IAN REDFORD

**Born:** Perth, 5 April 1960
**Rangers career:** 1980 to 1986
**Appearances and goals:**

| League | | FA Cup | | Lg Cup | | Europe | |
|---|---|---|---|---|---|---|---|
| **A** | **G** | **A** | **G** | **A** | **G** | **A** | **G** |
| 149/23 | 23 | 21/1 | 5 | 35/5 | 11 | 10/3 | 3 |

*Total appearances:* 215/32
*Total goals:* 42
**Scottish Cup:** 1980-81
**League Cup:** 1981-82; 1984-85

Rangers set a new record transfer fee between Scottish clubs when they paid Dundee £210,000 for Ian Redford's services in February 1980.

With Dundee, Redford won Scottish youth and Under-21 honours, and in 1978-79 helped the Dark Blues win a place in the Scottish Premier League after finishing as First Division Champions.

The son of a prosperous farmer in Perthshire, he made his Rangers debut in a 3-0 defeat of Morton and played in the final 13 games of that 1979-80 season.

During the course of the following season, it was Redford's dramatic last-minute equaliser against St Johnstone in the fourth round of the Scottish Cup that kept the Light Blues alive in the competition—in fact, he netted twice in a 3-3 draw. However, in the final against Dundee United, he achieved a certain notoriety with Rangers fans for his last-minute penalty miss, when his shot was hard and straight and bounced to safety off goalkeeper McAlpine's legs. Rangers made amends in the replay by winning 4-1.

In 1981-82, Redford scored four goals in the 8-1 League Cup victory over Raith Rovers, and he was outstanding throughout the club's run to the final, where they once again met Dundee United. The game was all-square at 1-1 with just a couple of minutes remaining, when Redford produced what turned out to be the winning goal.

Redford was a regular in the Rangers side for the next few seasons, and after being on the losing side in the Scottish Cup Final of 1981-82 and both of the domestic cup finals in 1982-83, he won another League Cup winners' medal in 1984-85, his last season with the club as the Gers beat—who else but Dundee United—1-0.

In fact, Dundee United were Ian Redford's next club, and his form for the Tannadice side alerted a number of sides south of the border. It was Ipswich Town boss John Duncan who acted quickest, taking the winger to Portman Road. Redford was a regular in the Suffolk club's side for the next three seasons, scoring 12 goals in 80 games.

After leaving the game for a spell, he returned to action in his native Scotland with Raith Rovers, but nowadays, Ian Redford, who was a founder of Fair Game Scotland, a leisure facility at Dunkeld based around salmon-fishing, plays golf with a handicap of two.

## FERNANDO RICKSEN

**Born:** Heerlen, Holland, 27 July 1976
**Rangers career:** 2000 to 2006
**Appearances and goals:**

| League | | FA Cup | | Lg Cup | | Europe | |
|---|---|---|---|---|---|---|---|
| **A** | **G** | **A** | **G** | **A** | **G** | **A** | **G** |
| 179/3 | 14 | 17 | 0 | 16/1 | 3 | 39 | 2 |

*Total appearances:* 251/4
*Total goals:* 19
**League Championships:** 2002-03; 2004-05
**Scottish Cup:** 2001-02; 2002-03
**League Cup:** 2001-02; 2002-03; 2004-05
**Honours:** 8 Holland caps

Rangers signed Fernando Ricksen from AZ67 Alkmaar in the summer of 2000, beating off competition from Ajax and other clubs from around Europe.

Fernando, who was named after the Abba song, started out with Roda JC as a youth player, but after growing unhappy about his lack of first team chances, he was quickly snapped up and signed professional terms with Fortuna Sittard. In his first season, the youth team he played in won the League before, the following season, he established himself in the senior side.

It wasn't long before his talent was spotted, and in 1997 Ricksen signed for AZ67 Alkmaar for a fee of around £750,000. He had great ambitions of being a central midfielder, although the club's new coach had other ideas, knowing that Ricksen was one of the best attacking right-backs he had ever seen.

Although a tough tackler and successful as a defender, Ricksen likes nothing better than to get forward and score goals—something he did well following his £3.6 million arrival. However, he did endure a difficult start to his Rangers career, culminating in him being substituted in the first-half of the 6-2 defeat by Celtic. There was also concern from many supporters with regard to Ricksen's somewhat fiery temperament and rumours about excessive alcohol consumption!

The departure of Dick Advocaat during the 2001-02 season appeared to give Ricksen a new lease of life, as he helped the Light Blues to League Cup and Scottish Cup triumphs under the management of Alex McLeish.

Ricksen, who was twice punished on the basis of video evidence after incidents on the pitch missed by match officials, also found himself in trouble with the law. In November 2002, he was fined £7,000 after attacking a neighbour who had complained about him letting off fireworks in the early hours of the morning. Just a month later, and the defender was given another fine and also banned from driving for a year after he drove his car into a lamppost on Christmas Day. Ricksen's behaviour also resulted in a sudden end to his international career after he allegedly kicked a hotel door while with the Dutch national team in Belarus.

He was, though, a key player in Rangers' 2002-03 treble success, forming a key partnership with Barry Ferguson and netting twice in the club's 4-0 defeat of Hearts at Tynecastle. Despite the departure of Ferguson and Lorenzo Amoruso and he himself suffering several injury problems the following season, he again proved a major player. He was ever-present in 2004-05, helping Rangers win the League Cup and the SPL title after a dramatic final day of the season. He was also given the captaincy for a large part of the season following an injury to goalkeeper Stefan Klos. Ricksen was later voted both Rangers Player of the Year and joint Scottish PFA players' Player of the Year along with Celtic's John Hartson.

He failed to sustain the standard set in the previous seasons in 2005-6 as Rangers finished the campaign without a trophy, although they did reach the last 16 of the UEFA Champions League.

An incident on Rangers' outbound flight to the pre-season camp in South Africa in the summer of 2006 led to Ricksen being sent home by new manager Paul le Guen. After a spell in the London-based Sporting Chance Clinic, he joined Zenit St Petersburg on a season-long loan, but within a matter of months the move had been made permanent, with Rangers receiving a fee of £1 million.

## BILLY RITCHIE

**Born:** Newtongrange, 11 September 1936
**Rangers career:** 1955 to 1967
**Appearances and goals:**

| League | | FA Cup | | Lg Cup | | Europe | |
|---|---|---|---|---|---|---|---|
| A | G | A | G | A | G | A | G |
| 207 | 0 | 37 | 0 | 65 | 0 | 30 | 0 |

*Total appearances:* 339

*Total goals:* 0
**League Championships:** 1962-63; 1963-64
**Scottish Cup:** 1961-62; 1962-63; 1963-64; 1965-66
**League Cup:** 1961-62; 1963-64; 1964-65
**Honours:** 1 Scotland cap

Goalkeeper Billy Ritchie was signed from Bathgate Thistle in August 1954, his career overlapping and eventually succeeding George Niven's, as he became the club's No.1 in one of the greatest of all Rangers teams, that of the early sixties.

Ritchie initially had to bide his time in the club's reserve team, and he played his first match in May 1957 in a Charity Cup-tie at home to Third Lanark. He secured a regular place in the Rangers side in the second half of the 1957-58 season as the Light Blues finished runners-up to Hearts. He also played in all of the club's matches in the run to the League Cup Final, but was replaced by Niven for the Final—a match Rangers lost 7-1 to Celtic!

National Service took him to Cyprus for the whole of the following season, and when he returned to Ibrox, he found George Niven's form was just too good to allow him back in the first team.

Following Niven's transfer to Partick Thistle, Ritchie found himself as the club's first-choice keeper, and for the next five years was an outstanding goalkeeper in an outstanding Rangers team. He was an undemonstrative keeper and was considered the 'quiet man' of the team, but he was also a solidly reliable goalkeeper who kept a clean sheet in every third game he played for Rangers.

In 1961-62 he helped Rangers to win both League and Scottish Cups, and was rewarded with full international honours when he came off the bench to replace Dunfermline Athletic's goalkeeper Eddie Connachan in the match against Uruguay at Hampden Park. His first touch of the ball was to pick it out of his own net in a 3-2 defeat. In terms of international football, Ritchie was certainly unlucky to be a contemporary of Spurs goalkeeper Bill Brown, who went on to win 28 caps for his country.

In 1962-63 he missed just one match—a 1-0 defeat to runners-up Kilmarnock—as Rangers won the League Championship and kept a clean sheet in the Scottish Cup Final when Celtic were beaten 3-0. The following season, Rangers not only retained the title but also completed the treble by winning both domestic cup competitions. Further successes in the cup competitions came when Rangers won the League Cup in 1964-65 and the Scottish Cup in 1965-66—with Celtic the defeated opposition on both occasions.

The last of his Rangers appearances was against Aberdeen in a League Cup semi-final at Hampden, a match that ended all-square at 2-2. Replaced by Norrie Martin, he remained at Ibrox for another year, before, like George Niven before him, Billy Ritchie was transferred to Partick Thistle.

# DAVID ROBERTSON

**Born:** Aberdeen, 17 October 1968
**Rangers career:** 1991 to 1997
**Appearances and goals:**

| League | | FA Cup | | Lg Cup | | Europe | |
|---|---|---|---|---|---|---|---|
| **A** | **G** | **A** | **G** | **A** | **G** | **A** | **G** |
| 182/1 | 15 | 26 | 3 | 18/1 | 1 | 22 | 0 |

*Total appearances:* 248/2
*Total goals:* 19
**League Championships:** 1991-92; 1992-93; 1993-94; 1994-95; 1995-96; 1996-97
**Scottish Cup:** 1991-92; 1992-93; 1995-96
**League Cup:** 1992-93; 1993-94; 1996-97
**Honours:** 3 Scotland caps

Signed in the summer of 1991 for a bargain £970,000, set at a transfer tribunal when his contract at Aberdeen expired, David Robertson won increasing admiration and favour from the Ibrox crowd as he proved to be a fiery competitor as well as a lightning-fast defender.

After bursting onto the scene with his home-town team Aberdeen in the mid-eighties, Robertson was the most consistent left-back in Scotland. During the course of the 1988-89 season he really endeared himself to Rangers fans as he was involved in a shocking mix-up with Dons keeper Theo Snelders when Aberdeen played Rangers in a superb Skol Cup Final at Hampden. A poor Robertson throw-in had the Dutch keeper in total confusion, and Ally McCoist nipped in to open the scoring as Rangers went on to win 3-2.

The very next season, Aberdeen returned to Hampden to face Rangers in the club's third successive League Cup Final showdown. This time he had the last laugh as two Paul Mason goals took the trophy to Pittodrie. More glory was to come his way as Aberdeen won the Scottish Cup after a thrilling penalty shoot-out with Celtic.

With Walter Smith eager to start accumulating Scots because of European restrictions, Rangers signed Robertson, after which it was one success after another for the quiet man of the club. There were few setbacks, although a red card in the opening minutes of the Scottish Cup semi-final at Hampden against Celtic in the 1991-92 season was a real low point. To make matters worse, the dismissal was earned for a foul on his close friend from their Aberdeen days, Joe Miller. No real damage was done, as the Light Blues won that match, and with Robertson back in the side beat Airdrie 2-1 in the final.

The next Treble-winning season emphasised Robertson's increasing importance through his sterling displays at home and in the club's glorious Champions League run. Sadly, he only won three full caps for Scotland, due in the main to the link-up at club and international level between Celtic's Tommy Boyd and John Collins.

Having won six successive League Championship medals as well as three League Cup and Scottish Cup medals, Robertson left Ibrox in the summer of 1997 to join Leeds United for a fee of £500,000.

The Elland Road club's boss George Graham, who had been tracking Robertson ever since he took over the reins of the Yorkshire club, feared the Rangers defender might move abroad for free as his contract was due to expire. He took a little while to adjust to the game in the Premiership, and was just finding his form when he tore a cartilage in training, which later forced him to part company with the club.

## MAURICE ROSS

**Born:** Dundee, 3 February 1981
**Rangers career:** 2000 to present
**Appearances and goals:**

| League | | FA Cup | | Lg Cup | | Europe | |
|---|---|---|---|---|---|---|---|
| **A** | **G** | **A** | **G** | **A** | **G** | **A** | **G** |
| 60/18 | 2 | 5/2 | 0 | 8/2 | 1 | 9/5 | 0 |

*Total appearances:* 82/27
*Total goals:* 3
**League Championships:** 2002-03; 2004-05
**Scottish Cup:** 2001-02; 2002-03
**League Cup:** 2002-03; 2004-05
**Honours:** 13 Scotland caps

Maurice Ross suffered more than his fair share of injuries during his time at Ibrox, having joined Rangers as trainee. He made his debut as a substitute for Claudio Reyna in a 7-1 thrashing of his home-town club Dundee at Dens Park in February 2000, before returning to the club's reserve side.

Ross was a star in the club's youth teams and captained the Under-21s to win the Championship in 2000-01. After establishing himself in the Rangers back four midway through the 2001-02 season, Ross won his first major honour when he helped the Light Blues lift the Scottish Cup, beating Celtic 3-2 in the final. Rangers had previously won that season's League Cup, but Ross hadn't won a regular place by then.

The then Scotland manager Berti Vogts took a chance on Ross, who is able to play in defence or on the right-side of midfield, and handed him an international call up when he'd only made a few senior appearances for the Gers. Ross made his debut for Scotland against the Korean Republic in May 2002, and went on to feature prominently in the team as they tried and failed to secure a place in the Euro 2004 Championships.

The following domestic season saw Ross score his first goal for the club in a 2-0 home win over Livingston, helping Rangers win the League title on goal difference from Celtic. He made appearances off the bench in both domestic cup finals as Rangers won the League Cup, beating Celtic 2-1, and gained the Scottish Cup with a 1-0 victory over Dundee.

Having signed a four-year contract with the Light Blues, he continued, injuries apart, to feature regularly in Alex McLeish's plans, and in 2003-04, netted his second goal for the club against Motherwell.

In 2004-05 he helped the Gers to yet another League Championship triumph, and success in the League Cup with a 5-1 demolition of Motherwell. In fact, Ross scored one of his only three goals for the club in that Hampden Park encounter. The defender, who has made 13 appearances for the national side, later moved to Sheffield Wednesday. Unable to make much of an impression, he was loaned to Wolves, with the deal later being made permanent. There followed a spell with Millwall before his latest move, to sign for the Norwegian club, Viking.

## BOBBY RUSSELL

**Born:** Glasgow, 11 February 1957
**Rangers career:** 1977 to 1987
**Appearances and goals:**

| League | | FA Cup | | Lg Cup | | Europe | |
|---|---|---|---|---|---|---|---|
| **A** | **G** | **A** | **G** | **A** | **G** | **A** | **G** |
| 218/32 | 31 | 37/2 | 8 | 50/5 | 6 | 25 | 1 |

*Total appearances:* 330/39
*Total goals:* 46
**League Championships:** 1977-78
**Scottish Cup:** 1977-78; 1978-79; 1980-81
**League Cup:** 1978-79; 1981-82; 1983-84; 1984-85

Bobby Russell, who arrived at Ibrox from Shettleston Juniors in 1977, was an extremely talented footballer, but though he was often selected for Scotland, injury each time denied him his cap.

Having scored on his Rangers debut in a pre-season friendly against Nairn County, Bobby Russell went on to help Rangers win both the League Championship and Scottish Cup in 1977-78, his first season in the side. In fact, the Light Blues completed the Treble, but Russell was forced to miss the League Cup Final through injury.

He helped Rangers retain the Scottish Cup the following season, although it took three matches for the Gers to beat Hibernian. He also picked up his first League Cup winners' medal after a 2-1 success over Aberdeen.

That 1978-79 season saw Bobby Russell score one of the most startling and audacious goals ever seen in European competition. In a second round Champions Cup match against PSV Eindhoven in October 1978, the Dutch side had come away from Ibrox with a goalless draw. In the second leg in Holland, PSV scored after just half a minute, but Rangers fought back and twice equalised to make the score 2-2. There were just three minutes remaining as the Dutch side pressed for the goal that would take them through—if it remained at 2-2, Rangers would go through on the away goal rule. But Johnstone's headed clearance was picked up by Smith who in turn fed McLean. The winger clipped a beautiful ball beyond the last two defenders, and Russell, coming in at speed, bent his shot round the advancing keeper for a goal of sheer brilliance. It was PSV's first defeat at home in any European match!

In 1980-81, Russell won his third Scottish Cup medal, scoring in the replayed final as Dundee United were beaten 4-1. Comparable in style to that great Spurs inside-forward John White, Russell went on to win three further League Cup winners' medals in a ten-year stay at Ibrox, before he left to continue his career with Motherwell in 1987.

A few eyebrows were raised, but Tommy McLean knew what he was doing as Russell proved to be another shrewd purchase. He scored a wonderful solo goal for Motherwell against Rangers in a 1-0 win at Fir Park in October 1989 as the Steelmen surged to the top of the Premier League. However, he was plagued by injury, and eventually the infrequency of his outings for Motherwell signalled his departure.

Bobby Russell went to Northern Ireland from Motherwell, playing at Coleraine. He then joined Ayr United in January 1993, but lasted only a couple of months, until knee problems finally forced him to retire.

## EDDIE RUTHERFORD

**Born:** Glasgow, 8 February 1921
**Rangers career:** 1946 to 1952
**Appearances and goals:**

| League | | FA Cup | | Lg Cup | | Europe | |
|---|---|---|---|---|---|---|---|
| A | G | A | G | A | G | A | G |
| 95 | 19 | 17 | 4 | 28 | 5 | - | - |

*Total appearances:* 140
*Total goals:* 28
**League Championships:** 1948-49; 1949-50
**Scottish Cup:** 1947-48; 1948-49; 1949-50
**League Cup:** 1946-47; 1948-49
**Honours:** 1 Scotland cap

Eddie Rutherford emerged during the Second World War, when having signed for Rangers from Mossvale Amateurs in the summer of 1941, he guested for Leeds United, Lincoln City and Bradford City. Also, in his early years with the Ibrox club, he was employed as a commercial traveller in the Glasgow area for a firm of chemists.

Though he was a natural outside-right, he was able to play on either flank, but with Willie Waddell firmly in place in the No.7 shirt, Rutherford became the club's outside-left in place of Jimmy Caskie, whose career was coming to an end. Though there were occasions when he looked most uncomfortable out wide on the left, he was well served by a succession of wing-halves who included Sammy Cox and Willie Rae and inside-left Jimmy Duncanson.

Rutherford made his league debut for the Light Blues midway through the 1946-47 season in a 2-1 home win over Queen of the South, going on to make a handful of appearances that season, and scored his first goal in a 5-0 home defeat of Clyde in the penultimate game of the campaign. A week later he was a member of the Rangers side that lifted the League Cup, beating Aberdeen 4-0 in the Final. He appeared on a much more regular basis the following season and helped the club win the Scottish Cup, defeating Morton 1-0 in the Final at Hampden Park.

In 1948-49, Rutherford was a member of the Rangers side that completed the Treble, pipping Dundee by a point to lift the Championship and defeating Clyde and Raith Rovers in the Scottish Cup and League Cup Finals respectively. His form that season led to him winning full international honours for Scotland, but he was on the losing side as France ran out 3-0 winners.

Rangers retained the title in 1949-50, with Rutherford scoring seven goals in 22 games, and creating many more for Thornton and Duncanson. The Gers also won the Scottish Cup for a third successive season, beating East Fife 3-0, but lost the chance of completing a second successive Treble when losing 2-1 to the Fifers in the League Cup semi-final.

Particularly dangerous when he cut inside on his right foot, Rutherford always gave the impression that he was enjoying his game.

In November 1951 he left Ibrox to join Hearts in an exchange deal involving Colin Liddell moving in the opposite direction. He did well at Tynecastle, helping to bring on some of the club's young attackers. However, knee injuries and a cartilage operation reduced his effectiveness, and early in 1955 he moved on to Raith Rovers. Rutherford later ended his career with Hamilton Academical before going to run a newsagency at Rutherglen.

## ALEX SCOTT

**Born:** Falkirk, 22 November 1936
**Rangers career:** 1954 to 1963
**Appearances and goals:**

| League | | FA Cup | | Lg Cup | | Europe | |
|---|---|---|---|---|---|---|---|
| A | G | A | G | A | G | A | G |
| 216 | 67 | 25 | 5 | 62 | 24 | 28 | 12 |

*Total appearances:* 331
*Total goals:* 108
**League Championships:** 1955-56; 1956-57; 1958-59; 1960-61
**Scottish Cup:** 1959-60
**League Cup:** 1960-61; 1961-62
**Honours:** 16 Scotland caps

Alex Scott was an outside-right of devastating pace and fearsome finishing power, and on his league debut against his home-town team Falkirk in March 1955, scored a hat-trick in a 4-1 win.

Six days later Rangers visited Highbury to play Arsenal and drew 3-3, with two of their goals scored in the opening quarter of the match by Alex Scott. His brilliant performance that day drew comparisons with the legendary Alex James.

Signed from Camelon Thistle in the Falkirk area, he was the perfect replacement for Willie Waddell, though he did have a rather strange running style, because in spite of his speed, his left arm stayed by his side and scarcely moved!

As well as helping Rangers win the League Championship in 1955-56, Scott netted another treble, this time in the 8-0 League Cup thrashing of Hamilton Academical. Scott went on to win four League Championship medals, winning his last one in 1960-61 when he scored his third and final hat-trick in a last day 7-3 win over Ayr United. Also that season, Scott won his first League Cup winners' medal, scoring his side's second goal in a 2-0 defeat of Kilmarnock in the Final.

Scott, who scored the only goal of the game on his international debut against Northern Ireland in November 1956, netted a hat-trick against the same opposition some five years later.

Scott was also a member of the Rangers side that lost the 1961 European Cup Winners Cup Final in Florence, when he scored the only Light Blues goal. Indeed he scored, in all, five goals en route to that final. He was also the scorer of Rangers' 5000th League goal in that Championship winning game against Ayr in April 1961.

In February 1963, Alex Scott left Rangers to join Everton for a fee of £40,000. It was one of the fiercest transfer battles of the decade. The flying winger had been pursued by a number of top Football League clubs when it became known that he was keen on a move south of the border. Everton and Spurs led the way with a long series of bids, offers and pledges before the Merseyside club won the race for his signature.

Known to Everton fans as 'Chico' because of his swarthy skin, Scott ended his first season at Goodison Park with a League Championship medal, having established himself as an integral part of the set up. Scott was a model of consistency—he was outstanding in the Merseyside club's run to the FA Cup Final in 1966 where they came from behind to beat Sheffield Wednesday 3-2. His peak was passing, however, and in September 1967 he returned to Scotland, joining Hibernian for £15,000.

He spent a couple of seasons at Easter Road, later ending his career with his home-town club before going into business with his younger brother James, who also played for Hibernian, Newcastle United and Scotland.

## JOCK SHAW

**Born:** Annathill, 29 November 1912
**Died:** 20 June 2000
**Rangers career:** 1946 to 1953
**Appearances and goals:**

| League | | FA Cup | | Lg Cup | | Europe | |
|---|---|---|---|---|---|---|---|
| **A** | **G** | **A** | **G** | **A** | **G** | **A** | **G** |
| 169 | 1 | 27 | 0 | 42 | 0 | - | - |

*Total appearances:* 238
*Total goals:* 1
**League Championships:** 1938-39; 1946-47; 1948-49; 1949-50
**Scottish Cup:** 1947-48; 1948-49; 1949-50
**League Cup:** 1946-47; 1948-49
**Honours:** 4 Scotland caps

Known as 'Tiger', Jock Shaw's tackling certainly had bite, and his uncompromising style made him one of the most feared and respected of opponents.

Rangers' legendary manager Bill Struth signed Jock Shaw from Airdrie for a fee of just £2,000 in the summer of 1938, and he made his debut at left-back on the opening day of the 1938-39 season in a 3-3 draw with St Johnstone. Missing just two games, he won a League Championship winners' medal in his first season with the club, but then the outbreak of the Second World War forced the abandonment of Scottish League fixtures until 1946-47.

During the hostilities, Shaw played in two wartime internationals in 1941 and 1943, both at Hampden and both against England, and in Victory Internationals in 1945 and 1946. Indeed, he and his brother David of Hibernian formed the full-back pairing in the 1946 Victory International against England which Scotland won 1-0. Shaw played in four of his country's international matches during 1947, but was succeeded over the next couple of years in the national team by his younger brother.

Shaw played 28 of the 30 League games as Rangers won the first peacetime League Championship. He also got a winners' medal in the new League Cup competition as Aberdeen were beaten 4-0 in the Final. The following season

*Rangers legends Jock Shaw (left) and Willie Woodburn watch players at the Albion training ground in Glasgow (www.snspix.com)*

he won a Scottish Cup winners' medal following a 1-0 win over Morton, and scored what was his only goal for the club with a penalty in a 3-0 win over Airdrie.

Jock Shaw was club captain, and during his time at Ibrox collected four League Championship medals, three Scottish Cup and two League Cup winners medals. Included in that array of honours was the Treble in 1948–49—achieved in his 38th year. Undoubtedly there would have been more but for the war.

Jock Shaw was 42 years old when he finally retired. This came about following an extensive Rangers tour of Canada and the United States in the summer of 1954. The fact that he played at such a high level for so long was a tribute to his fitness, sustained over so many years.

He later became trainer, managing Rangers' third team, and also worked on the Ibrox club's groundstaff. Future stars such as the young John Greig, Sandy Jardine and winger Willie Henderson all came under his charge.

## BOBBY SHEARER

**Born:** Hamilton, 29 December 1931
**Died:** 5 November 2006
**Rangers career:** 1955 to 1965

**Appearances and goals:**

| League | | FA Cup | | Lg Cup | | Europe | |
|---|---|---|---|---|---|---|---|
| **A** | **G** | **A** | **G** | **A** | **G** | **A** | **G** |
| 268 | 2 | 37 | 0 | 72 | 2 | 30 | 0 |

*Total appearances:* 407

*Total goals:* 4

**League Championships:** 1956-57; 1958-59; 1960-61; 1962-63; 1963-64

**Scottish Cup:** 1961-62; 1962-63; 1963-64

**League Cup:** 1960-61; 1961-62; 1963-64

**Honours:** 4 Scotland caps

---

Nicknamed 'Captain Cutlass', Bobby Shearer was a fierce-tackling full-back, whose never-say-die attitude made him an ideal candidate for Rangers' captain, which he eventually became.

A red-haired firebrand of a defender, Bobby Shearer was signed from Hamilton Academical, where his father was head groundsman and for almost a decade was a good if unpolished full-back for Rangers. During his time with the Accies, Shearer had showed his versatility by playing in every position except goal.

He made his Rangers debut in a 4-0 win at Airdrie midway through the 1955-56 season, a match in which Sammy Baird netted a hat-trick. Appointed captain, he led Rangers to the first of five League Championships under his

*Bobby Shearer in his later career as a businessman (www.snspix.com)*

leadership in 1956-57 and formed a formidable full-back partnership with Eric Caldow.

He was a leader both on and off the pitch and was hugely influential on the great John Greig who came into the Light Blues' side under his tutelage. He was also a death-or-glory, take-no-prisoners defender who played for Rangers in the 1961 European Cup Winners' Cup Final when the Ibrox club lost 4-1 on aggregate to Fiorentina.

Though his lack of pace occasionally left him exposed at higher levels of the game—on his full international debut he was part of the Scotland team beaten 9-3 by England at Wembley in April 1961—few Rangers players have collected more trophies than Bobby Shearer.

He led the club to five League titles, three Scottish Cup Final victories and to success in three League Cup Finals also. He was captain when the Gers won the Treble in 1963-64—only the second time it had happened. The clean sweep was clinched with a remarkable 3-1 Scottish Cup Final win over Dundee when Rangers scored twice in the dying moments. He was a key protagonist in the club's early 1960s side which is still revered all over the world as one of the best—if not the best—in the club's history.

Shearer, who played in 407 games for Rangers including a run of 165 consecutive matches, later joined Queen of the South as player-coach before in January 1967 becoming manager of Third Lanark. After the club folded the following season, Shearer took charge of his former club Hamilton Academicals before leaving to concentrate on his business interests, which included bus-hiring and building firms.

## BILLY SIMPSON

**Born:** Belfast, date not found

**Rangers career:** 1950 to 1959

**Appearances and goals:**

| League | | FA Cup | | Lg Cup | | Europe | |
|---|---|---|---|---|---|---|---|
| A | G | A | G | A | G | A | G |
| 172 | 113 | 23 | 15 | 38 | 35 | 6 | 2 |

Total appearances: 239

Total goals: 165

**League Championships:** 1952-53; 1955-56; 1956-57

**Scottish Cup:** 1952-53

**Honours:** 12 Ireland caps

Billy Simpson was a terrific striker who cost a club record fee of £11,500 from Linfield on the recommendation of Rangers great Tory Gillick. He could play at inside-forward equally well, but it was through the middle where he was at his best as his 163 goals prove.

With the careers of Gillick, Jimmy Duncanson and Billy Williamson all drawing to a close, Rangers needed to strengthen their forward line. A number of players were tried but lacked the standards required by the Ibrox club. After Rangers boss Bill Struth had been alerted to Simpson's talents, he sent Tory Gillick to Belfast to assess him. Gillick reportedly favourably and Simpson became one of only a handful of players to score a hundred or more League goals since the Second World War.

He netted a hat-trick on Christmas Eve 1950, in what was only his second game, as East Fife were beaten 5-0. He went on to score 13 goals in 19 games, including four in the penultimate game of the season in a 5-0 rout of Third Lanark. Injuries hampered his progress the following season, but in 1952-53 he was back to help Rangers to a League and Scottish Cup double. He scored 21 goals in as many League games, including a hat-trick in a 6-4 win at Clyde and all four goals in a 4-0 home win over St Mirren. Simpson also scored the only goal of the replayed Scottish Cup Final against Aberdeen.

Simpson was not one of the most physical players you could imagine, not powerful in the slightest, but if he lacked polish, he certainly had courage to spare. Simpson was, above all else, a goalscorer, and there were many times when he would risk injury to reach the ball—many times netting chances and half-chances in the six-yard box.

Having helped Rangers to another League title in 1955-56, Simpson helped the Gers retain the Championship the following season when he again netted 21 goals. His single most important goal for Rangers may well have been with his head against Hearts at Tynecastle towards the end of that 1956-57 campaign. It broke the Jam Tarts and set up Rangers' Championship after they had been seven points behind Hearts in the final straight.

Simpson was a magnificent header of the ball, and his 100th goal for the club saw him score with a powerfully placed diving header in the 3-2 defeat by Hearts in October 1957. Having netted a hat-trick in the opening League Cup game in a 6-0 thrashing of St Mirren, Simpson scored in the Final, but was on the losing side as Celtic ran out 7-1 winners! In November 1957, Simpson scored the winning goal for Northern Ireland against England at Wembley.

In 1958-59, his last season at Ibrox, Simpson scored four goals for Rangers for the third time as Hibernian were beaten 4-0. He also netted a hat-trick in the 6-0 League Cup defeat of Raith Rovers before being transferred to Stirling Albion.

# DAVE SMITH

**Born:** Aberdeen, 14 November 1943
**Rangers career:** 1966 to 1974
**Appearances and goals:**

| League | | FA Cup | | Lg Cup | | Europe | |
|---|---|---|---|---|---|---|---|
| **A** | **G** | **A** | **G** | **A** | **G** | **A** | **G** |
| 187/8 | 8 | 28/2 | 0 | 36/6 | 2 | 31/5 | 3 |

*Total appearances:* 282/21
*Total goals:* 13
**European Cup Winners Cup:** 1971-72
**Honours:** 2 Scotland caps

Dave Smith was a superb cultured left-half, and was already an international player when he signed for Rangers from Aberdeen in the summer of 1966.

The brother of Dundee United's tough-tackling centre-half, Doug Smith, he began his career with his home-town club Aberdeen, where his displays for the Pittodrie club led to him winning selection for the Under-23 and Scottish League XI before winning the first of his two full caps against Holland.

He scored on his Rangers league debut on the opening day of the 1966-67 season as Partick Thistle were beaten 6-1, and went on to be an ever-present as the Light Blues finished as runners-up to Celtic. He also helped the Gers reach the League Cup Final, but once again the Hoops got the better of them, albeit by the game's only goal. It was a similar story the following season, with Rangers finishing two points behind League Champions Celtic. The 1968-69 season was no different, as Rangers were once again runners-up to the Parkhead club and lost to them 4-0 in the final of the Scottish Cup.

Dave Smith was an elegant player, succeeding Jim Baxter in the Rangers side, but he never quite had the acclaim he should have had and he certainly should have represented Scotland more often—as it was he made just one more appearance for the national side, once again against Holland. His precise passing of the ball made him one of the outstanding players in the Scottish game of his time.

Though he failed to win any of the honours on offer in the Scottish League and Cup competitions, he was a member of the Rangers side that won the European Cup Winners' Cup Final in 1971-72 when he played as a sweeper in the club's 3-2 victory over Dynamo Moscow.

Having appeared in over 300 games for Rangers, Smith left Ibrox to sign for Arbroath for a fee of just £12,000—a snip for a player whose signature when he joined Rangers was one of the most sought after in the game.

He hadn't been at Gayfield Park long when he was made player-coach, but just over a season later, he was on the move again, this time to Berwick

Rangers as the club's player-manager. He spent a little over four years with the Borderers, leading them to the 1978-79 Second Division Championship and to the following season's Scottish Cup quarter-final before joining Peterhead in a similar capacity.

Dave Smith also had a spell playing in the NASL for Los Angles Aztecs and in South Africa.

## GORDON SMITH

**Born:** Kilwinning, 29 December 1954
**Rangers career:** 1977 to 1980 and 1982-83
**Appearances and goals:**

| League | | FA Cup | | Lg Cup | | Europe | |
|---|---|---|---|---|---|---|---|
| **A** | **G** | **A** | **G** | **A** | **G** | **A** | **G** |
| 86/14 | 35 | 15/3 | 1 | 20 | 12 | 15/1 | 3 |

Total appearances: 136/21
Total goals: 51
**League Championships:** 1977-78
**Scottish Cup:** 1977-78; 1978-79
**League Cup:** 1977-78; 1978-79

One of the club's biggest bargain signings, Gordon Smith had arrived at Ibrox from Kilmarnock for £65,000 in August 1977 as an outside-left, but manager Jock Wallace made him into a deep left-sided midfielder, or alternatively, an out-and-out striker.

Smith had pedigree too: his great-grandfather 'Mattha' Smith had won Scottish Cup medals with Kilmarnock in 1920 and as captain nine years later.

Smith contributed greatly to the club's treble-winning season of 1977-78, his 20 goals in 34 league starts helping Rangers win the League Championship, two points clear of runners-up Aberdeen. He netted a hat-trick in the 6-1 League Cup victory over the Dons and then scored the winner in the final as Celtic were beaten 2-1. He failed to score in the Scottish Cup Final, but goals from McDonald and Johnstone were enough to defeat Aberdeen 2-1. Smith had never been known as a goalscorer before, but his partnership with Derek Johnstone tore defences apart—Johnstone scoring 37 goals and Smith 27.

He played an important part in Rangers' European Championships and domestic Cup campaigns in 1978-79, helping the Light Blues beat Hibernian over three matches to retain the Scottish Cup and defeat Aberdeen 2-1 in the League Cup Final. A Scottish Under-21 international, Smith came extremely close to winning full international honours, but it wasn't to be, and after the club failed to retain either of the Cups and dropped down to

*Rangers player-manager Graeme Souness in his final game as a player—a 2-0 victory in the League over Dunfermline in 1990 (www.snspix.com)*

fifth place in the League, he opted for a move to Brighton and Hove Albion for an astonishing fee of £400,000.

During his first season with the Seagulls, Smith netted a 19-minute hat-trick against Coventry City, finishing with 10 goals in 38 games. After a disappointing 1981-82 campaign he was back to his best, and though the south coast club lost their top flight status, they reached the FA Cup Final where they played Manchester United. He scored the game's opening goal after 13 minutes, but in extra-time he was guilty of missing the chance that would most surely have given Albion the Cup. Ten yards out and completely unmarked, Smith took Robinson's pass, but his shot struck the legs of Gary Bailey who then dived on the ball to prevent Smith getting to the rebound.

Smith was recalled to Rangers in controversial circumstances on loan, only a matter of days before the League Cup Final against Celtic, and put straight into the team. Rangers lost 2-1—it was a gamble by John Greig which did not come off.

After spells with Manchester City and Oldham Athletic, Smith played in Austria and Switzerland before running his own insurance and financial consultancy in Glasgow, advising Scottish footballers on investments.

## GRAEME SOUNESS

**Born:** Edinburgh, 6 May 1953
**Rangers career:** 1986 to 1990
**Appearances and goals:**

| League | | FA Cup | | Lg Cup | | Europe | |
|---|---|---|---|---|---|---|---|
| A | G | A | G | A | G | A | G |
| 38/12 | 3 | 2/3 | 0 | 6/3 | 2 | 9 | 0 |

*Total appearances:* 55/18
*Total goals:* 5
**League Championships:** 1986-87
**Honours:** 54 Scotland caps

Graeme Souness did not play that often for the Light Blues, but he was an exceptional, inspirational player whose mark on the club's history is indelible. He revolutionised both Rangers and Scottish football with his signings and success, bringing the title back to Ibrox after nine long years.

He started out with Tottenham Hotspur, but with established midfielders of the quality of Mullery, Perryman and Peters at White Hart Lane, the young Souness grew frustrated. After a spell playing for Montreal Olympic in the NASL, he walked out on the club before Spurs allowed him to join Middlesbrough. At the end of his first season at Ayresome Park, Boro were promoted to the First Division, and during his stay in the north-east, he developed into one of the game's most influential performers of all time.

In January 1978 he joined Bob Paisley's Liverpool for £352,000—then a record deal between Football League clubs. Teaming up with Kenny Dalglish he helped lay the foundation stone of the club's success over the next decade. During the 1980-81 European Cup campaign, he netted hat-tricks in the wins over Oulu Palloseura of Finland and CSKA Sofia of Bulgaria. He continued to score some vital goals, perhaps none more so than the one that beat Everton in the 1984 League Cup Final replay. Replacing Phil Thompson as skipper, he led the Reds to three successive titles and League Cups and one European Cup, becoming the most successful captain in the club's history.

In June 1984 he joined Italian giants Sampdoria, but after two quiet seasons, he was appointed player-manager of Rangers. His Rangers career on the pitch didn't get off to the best of starts, as he was sent off on his debut at Hibernian for kicking Hibs forward George McCluskey. Hibs had the last laugh, winning 2-1.

Graeme Souness is remembered more for his management skills rather than his on-field antics, and won a piece of silverware every year he was the Ibrox boss. He also brought some exceptional players to the club—England internationals Terry Butcher and Chris Woods arrived in the summer of 1986, and these brilliant signings helped end the club's nine-year Championship famine.

As the trophies kept coming, so did the talented English-based players. Trevor Steven, Gary Stevens and Ray Wilkins all left promising careers south of the border to join the Rangers' cause along with one of Scotland's favourite sons, Richard Gough. But perhaps Souness' biggest transfer was the acquisition of ex-Celtic star Mo Johnston. Partnering both McCoist and Hateley in two League Championship-winning campaigns, his signing had been another Souness masterstroke.

A part-owner of Rangers, Souness was still striving for the European Champions Cup when he left Ibrox in April 1991 to replace Kenny Dalglish as Liverpool manager. After the shock of undergoing major heart surgery, he led the Reds to the one trophy he had failed to capture as a player, the FA Cup.

After parting company with Liverpool, he managed Turkish side Galatasaray but was sacked after winning the Championship! He later managed Southampton and Torino before taking over the reins of Blackburn Rovers and leading the club to promotion to the Premiership. He then saw his side beat Spurs to win the League Cup, but later left Ewood Park to manage Newcastle United, a position he left in 2006. He is currently employed as a television analyst on Ireland's RTE.

# GARY STEVENS

**Born:** Barrow, 27 March 1963
**Rangers career:** 1988 to 1994
**Appearances and goals:**

| League | | FA Cup | | Lg Cup | | Europe | |
|---|---|---|---|---|---|---|---|
| A | G | A | G | A | G | A | G |
| 186/1 | 8 | 22 | 1 | 22 | 0 | 14 | 0 |

*Total appearances:* 244/1
*Total goals:* 9
**League Championships:** 1988-89; 1989-90; 1990-91; 1991-92; 1993-94
**Scottish Cup:** 1991-92
**League Cup:** 1988-89; 1990-91; 1993-94
**Honours:** 46 England caps

---

Gary Stevens' contribution to 'Nine-in-a-row' and to Rangers has somehow been completely underrated—perhaps because he was a full-back, perhaps because there were so many glamour players when he was merely a superbly reliable professional.

With his first club Everton, Stevens won an FA Cup winners' medal in 1984 and a League Championship medal in 1985, and was a member of the Everton side that won the European Cup Winners' Cup that same year, beating Rapid Vienna 3-1 in the final in Rotterdam.

Along with Lineker, Reid and Steven, he was one of the Everton quartet in England's team which reached the 1986 World Cup quarter-finals, but then he suffered an injury which kept him out of the first half of the Merseyside club's League Championship-winning season of 1986-87.

Possessing one of the game's longest throws, he became increasingly effective in attack as his all-round expertise developed. A series of niggling injuries in 1987-88 plus a difference of opinion with manager Colin Harvey saw Stevens leave Goodison Park for Rangers for a fee of £1.25 million in the summer of 1988.

He took some time to settle into the Scottish game and made few friends when he was clearly responsible for Celtic's winning goal in the 1989 Scottish Cup Final. His faulty back-pass allowed Joe Miller to steal possession and score the game's only goal.

However, in a most successful Rangers career, his time at Ibrox revolves around statistics; he was, amazingly enough, Graeme Souness' 20th signing in two seasons, and scored the first goal of Rangers' Nine-in-a-Row against Hamilton Academical on 13 August 1988—his debut. It is not just quality that managers pray for when they sign a player, but reliability, and Gary Stevens provided that by consistently playing football at the back and asking too many questions of most teams with athletic charges up the right touchline.

During his six years at Ibrox, before a £350,000 transfer to Tranmere Rovers in 1994, no one made more League appearances than Stevens, who missed only three games in his first four seasons. Even when Nine-in-a-Row finally arrived, three years later, only Richard Gough had made more League appearances during that run than this consistent defender.

He spent a further four seasons on the Wirral where, apart from a spell when he suffered a badly broken forearm, he missed very few games. He had appeared in 150 League and Cup games before Rovers released him in the summer of 1998, after which he decided to retire.

## COLIN STEIN

**Born:** Linlithgow, 10 May 1947
**Rangers career:** 1968 to 1973 and 1975 to 1977
**Appearances and goals:**

| League | | FA Cup | | Lg Cup | | Europe | |
|---|---|---|---|---|---|---|---|
| A | G | A | G | A | G | A | G |
| 123/5 | 64 | 20 | 9 | 31/2 | 14 | 25 | 10 |

*Total appearances:* 199/7
*Total goals:* 97
**League Cup:** 1970-71; 1975-76
**European Cup Winners Cup:** 1971-72
**Honours:** 21 Scotland caps

---

Colin Stein was the subject of the first six-figure transfer between Scottish clubs when he joined the Ibrox club from Hibernian in October 1968 for £100,000, and the bustling striker was a big favourite with the Rangers fans.

He could certainly score goals, and he famously netted Hibs' fifth goal in the 5-0 defeat of Napoli in the 1967-68 Fairs Cup. In fact, the 1967-68 season was full of rich pickings for Stein, who finished the campaign as Hibs' top scorer with 29 goals—not bad for a player who started out as a left-back!

Stein started his Rangers career in style, netting hat-tricks in each of his first two League games for the club as the Gers won 5-0 at Arbroath and then defeated Hibs 6-1 at Ibrox. He also netted a third treble towards the end of the campaign as Clyde were beaten 6-0. Though injuries hampered his progress towards the end of that campaign, he had scored 13 goals in 18 games as Rangers finished runners-up to Celtic.

Stein represented Scotland on 21 occasions, scoring 10 goals—four of which came in a World Cup qualifying match against Cyprus in May 1969.

An old-fashioned centre-forward, Stein had his best season in terms of goals scored in 1969-70 with 24 goals in 33 games, including another hat-trick in the 5-3 home win over Kilmarnock. One of the most popular strikers

*Colin Stein celebrates after scoring against Dynamo Moscow in the final of the 1972 European Cup Winners' Cup (www.snspix.com)*

to play for the club, he won a League Cup winners medal in 1970-71 when a Derek Johnstone goal was enough to beat Celtic. He unfortunately had a rather short fuse, and this resulted in him being sent off several times in his career.

After playing a major part in the club's European Cup Winners' Cup triumph, when he scored in the 3-2 final defeat of Dynamo Moscow in Barcelona, Stein was transferred to Coventry City for £90,000 plus Quinton Young, a former Ayr United winger.

He had some initial success at Highfield Road, scoring 12 goals in 35 games, and though he struggled to find the net as often in 1973-74, he did net a hat-trick in a 5-1 League Cup defeat of Darlington. His form for the Sky Blues led to him adding another four Scottish caps to his collection. However, in February 1995, when it appeared that Coventry could no longer maintain the transfer instalments, Stein rejoined Rangers.

It was to prove a fairytale return for the popular striker, as he scored the goal that gave Rangers a 1-1 draw at Hibernian and in doing so clinched the club's first League Championship for 11 years.

During the 1977-78 season he had a spell on loan with Kilmarnock, but at the end of that campaign he decided to end his involvement with the game. He later worked as a joiner.

# WILLIE THORNTON

**Born:** Winchburgh, 3 March 1920
**Died:** August 1991
**Rangers career:** 1936 to 1954
**Appearances and goals:**

| League | | FA Cup | | Lg Cup | | Europe | |
|---|---|---|---|---|---|---|---|
| A | G | A | G | A | G | A | G |
| 219 | 139 | 34 | 21 | 50 | 29 | - | - |

*Total appearances:* 303
*Total goals:* 189
**League Championships:** 1938-39; 1946-47; 1948-49; 1949-50
**Scottish Cup:** 1947-48; 1948-49; 1949-50
**League Cup:** 1946-47; 1948-49
**Honours:** 7 Scotland caps

---

The first post-war Rangers player to break the 100-goal barrier, Willie Thornton joined the Gers as a 16-year-old, and his debut in a 1-0 win at Partick Thistle in January 1937 made him one of the youngest ever Light Blues.

He appeared more often the following season before establishing himself as a first team regular in 1938-39, a season which brought him his first hat-trick against Motherwell and the first of his four League Championship medals. The war then interrupted his career and found him serving in the British Army's only surviving private regiment, the Duke of Atholl's Scottish Horse, and ended with the player honoured for gallantry in the Sicilian campaign.

Football returned and normal service was hastily resumed—Rangers retaining the League Championship and beating Aberdeen 4-0 in the final of the League Cup. That season, Thornton scored 18 goals in 25 league games, netting hat-tricks in the away wins over Falkirk and Hamilton and the home thrashing of Third Lanark.

In 1947-48, Thornton and his closest friend, right-winger Willie Waddell, were involved in the Scottish Cup semi-final against Hibernian, a game played in front of a staggering 143,570 people. They saw the tie decided by a solitary Willie Thornton goal—a diving header from a Waddell cross. The Light Blues duly went on to win the final against Morton as well.

His form led to him representing the Scottish League XI and winning his first full cap against Wales. Though he wasn't as successful as Scottish fans would have hoped during his time as a full international, he helped the Ibrox club win the treble in 1948-49 when he scored 34 goals in all competitions. This total included a hat-trick on the final day of the League campaign in a 4-1 win at Albion Rovers which gave the Gers the title and all three goals against East Fife in the Scottish Cup semi-final. Rangers retained the League title and Scottish Cup the following season, but East Fife got their revenge in the League Cup semi-final.

Thornton, who gave Rangers lengthy and loyal service, was voted Scotland's Player of the Year in 1952. Two years later he hung up his boots and went into management, initially at Dundee and Partick Thistle, before returning to Ibrox as assistant-manager to David White.

When White moved on, Thornton renewed the double act as he was reunited with Waddell who took over the managerial reins. In fact, during the crossover, Thornton was briefly in charge—winning both of his matches to become the only Rangers boss with a 100% record!

Before he died in August 1991, Willie Thornton also became custodian of the Trophy Room at Ibrox and was a perfect match-day host in, of course, the Thornton Suite. In his time with Rangers, Willie Thornton broke records galore and left us with his own record that will never be matched.

## WILLIE WADDELL

**Born:** Forth, 7 March 1921
**Rangers career:** 1938 to 1955
**Appearances and goals:**

| League | | FA Cup | | Lg Cup | | Europe | |
|---|---|---|---|---|---|---|---|
| **A** | **G** | **A** | **G** | **A** | **G** | **A** | **G** |
| 196 | 37 | 32 | 4 | 68 | 15 | - | - |

*Total appearances:* 296
*Total goals:* 56
**League Championships:** 1938-39; 1946-47; 1948-49; 1952-53
**Scottish Cup:** 1948-49; 1952-53
**Honours:** 17 Scotland caps

One of the most formidable characters in the history of Rangers Football Club, few men can have made a greater or more lasting contribution than Willie Waddell.

From the time he played for Rangers in a reserve game against Partick Thistle at Firhill at the age of 15 in 1936, until he retired in the eighties, Waddell had been player, manager, managing director/vice-chairman, director/consultant and, finally, an honorary director of the club. All this was over a span of some fifty years!

During his early days at Ibrox, Waddell was farmed out to Strathclyde Juniors by manager Bill Struth in an attempt to help him gain experience. He turned professional in May 1938, and in making his debut a few months later in a friendly, scored the only goal of the game. A week later he played in his first League game, helping Rangers to a 4-1 win over Ayr United. He went on to play in 27 games that season, scoring seven goals as Rangers won the League Championship.

He seemed destined for a most illustrious career, when the 1939-40 Scottish League season was abandoned after only five matches because of

*Rangers manager Willie Waddell (right) in 1970, with assistant Willie Thornton*
*(www.snspix.com)*

war. Having broken into one of the great Rangers teams, he could also have looked forward to a lengthy international run.

Rangers played in area divisional leagues during the hostilities, and Willie Waddell was a regular and influential member of the Light Blues side. The club carried off all seven league titles, and it was during this time that Waddell scored the first of his two hat-tricks for Rangers, against Third Lanark in August 1942.

When League football resumed, Waddell was a member of the Rangers side that retained the title and scored the goal that beat Hibernian in the new League Cup semi-final. He missed out on the final itself as Rangers defeated Aberdeen 4-0. He didn't appear in the Scottish Cup Final win against Morton the following season, though he had played a crucial part in the semi-final win over Hibernian.

His Cup Final hard luck story continued in 1948-49, when he missed the League Cup Final win over Raith Rovers. He had, though, in an earlier round netted a hat-trick against Clyde. However that season, as Rangers won the treble, he did win his first major Cup Winners' medal as Clyde were beaten 4-1 in the Scottish Cup Final.

Though his well-placed crosses brought Willie Thornton many goals, Waddell could be a powerful finisher himself. And perhaps the most important goal he ever scored was the one that won the League title for Rangers in 1952-53. Waddell had won his second Scottish Cup medal eight days earlier as Aberdeen were beaten 1-0 in a replayed final, but Rangers needed a point at Queen of the South on the final day of the campaign to take the Championship. With quarter of an hour remaining they were trailing 1-0, but up popped Waddell to make it 1-1, and so Rangers pipped Hibernian on goal average.

Capped 17 times by Scotland, having scored from the penalty-spot on his debut against Wales, he created numerous chances for his team-mates, and when Scotland beat England 3-1 at Wembley in April 1949, it was Waddell's inch-perfect cross that allowed Lawrie Reilly to head home his side's third goal.

At the end of his playing days, he became manager of Kilmarnock, helping them win the League Championship in 1964-65 and finish runners-up on four occasions. Killie also reached a Scottish Cup Final and two League Cup Finals, but were never on the winning side.

His period as Rangers manager was not only a time of success, but also of disaster. In 1971, 66 supporters who had gone to spend an afternoon watching the New Year's Old Firm match, died in a stadium staircase crush at Ibrox and a further 145 were injured. Waddell regarded that tragedy— and the imperative need to prevent it ever happening again—as almost his life's mission.

As a manager he had the judgement and faith to introduce youth into his teams with spectacular results. Of course the European Cup Winners' Cup victory of 1972 in Barcelona will always be his high point, but in 1970-71 he brought Rangers their first trophy in four and a half years with the League Cup. After the success against Moscow Dynamo, Waddell handed over the reins to his assistant, the first hands-on track-suited football coach in Rangers' history—Jock Wallace.

## ROD WALLACE

**Born:** Lewisham, 2 October 1969
**Rangers career:** 1998 to 2001
**Appearances and goals:**

| League | | FA Cup | | Lg Cup | | Europe | |
|---|---|---|---|---|---|---|---|
| A | G | A | G | A | G | A | G |
| 73/4 | 41 | 10/1 | 4 | 6 | 3 | 24/2 | 7 |

Total appearances: 113/7
Total goals: 55
**League Championships:** 1998-99; 1999-2000
**Scottish Cup:** 1998-99; 1999-2000
**League Cup:** 1998-99

A small but skilful forward, Rod Wallace signed for Southampton in 1986 along with his twin brother Ray—elder brother Danny Wallace had already become an established member of the Saints' first team.

On 22 October 1988, his two brothers Danny and Ray lined up alongside him in the Southampton team in a match at The Dell against Sheffield Wednesday—this was the first time three brothers had played in the same team in English professional top flight football. The following year he represented England at Under-21 level, and after he had scored 45 goals in 128 games, fellow First Division side Leeds United signed him for £1.6 million in the summer of 1991.

A year later, he helped the Yorkshire club win the League Championship. Wallace became an integral part of the Leeds squad for the next seven years, and was often found playing as an out-and-out striker or in a more wide position on the flanks. He won the 1993-94 Goal of the Season competition with a mazy dribble against Tottenham Hotspur. But after Howard Wilkinson left Leeds, Wallace's future looked bleak. His contract with the Elland Road club was due to expire in the summer of 1998 and this resulted in a Bosman transfer move north to ply his trade with Rangers.

His initial impact with Leeds was repeated at Ibrox, as the Light Blues won the domestic treble. Wallace himself netted a mighty 27 goals throughout the course of that 1998-99 campaign. Having scored on his debut on the opening day of the season—albeit a 2-1 defeat at Hearts—he netted 19 goals in the League including a hat-trick in a 5-0 win at Kilmarnock. Also that season, he scored the only goal of the Scottish Cup Final against Celtic and helped Rangers lift the League Cup with a 2-1 defeat of St Johnstone.

He added to his silverware the following season as Rangers retained the League title and Scottish Cup. Wallace netted 17 goals in 25 starts in the League, including another treble in a 6-2 home win over Motherwell, and helped the Gers beat Aberdeen 4-0 in the Scottish Cup Final. He seemed to drift out of Dick Advocaat's plans at Rangers, and only featured sporadically in the 2000-01 campaign before being released on a free transfer at the end of the season.

Numerous clubs were linked with Wallace, but in the end it was Premiership new boys Bolton Wanderers who snapped up the star in September 2001. He scored on his debut at Blackburn and managed to net other goals including one against his former club Southampton, but was unhappy on only being offered a one-year contract and joined Gillingham.

His time with the Gills was blighted by a succession of injuries, and at the end of the 2003-04 season, he announced his retirement. The summer of 2004 saw him return to Southampton in a one-off benefit game organised for elder brother Danny, who has been diagnosed with Multiple Sclerosis.

# MARK WALTERS

**Born:** Birmingham, 2 June 1964
**Rangers career:** 1987 to 1991
**Appearances and goals:**

| League | | FA Cup | | Lg Cup | | Europe | |
|---|---|---|---|---|---|---|---|
| **A** | **G** | **A** | **G** | **A** | **G** | **A** | **G** |
| 101/5 | 32 | 15 | 6 | 13 | 12 | 10 | 1 |

*Total appearances:* 139/5

*Total goals:* 51

**League Championships:** 1988-89; 1989-90; 1990-91
**League Cup:** 1988-89; 1990-91
**Honours:** 1 England cap

The first black player to play for Rangers in fifty years, Mark Walters was an early prototype for the unstoppable wide play of Brian Laudrup, but long before the Dane came on the scene it was Walters's special knack of tormenting Celtic which won the fans over. Sadly, he found some of his work in Scotland more difficult and less enjoyable because his arrival unearthed some despicable racism in the game, but Walters still stayed for a profitable four-year stretch.

Walters began his career with Aston Villa, making his debut at the tender age of 17 against Leeds United. Emerging as one of the country's most exciting attacking wingers, he won recognition for England at Under-21 level and over the next few years scored some brilliant goals. However, in 1986-87 it all started to go wrong, and under new manager Billy McNeill he was in and out of the side. Though he was restored to the team when Graham Taylor took over, he opted for a £550,000 move north of the border to Rangers.

Due to English clubs being banned from European competitions, teams such as Rangers, managed by Graeme Souness, were finding it easier to attract English players, and he signed a number of internationals like Terry Butcher, Gary Stevens, Chris Woods and Ray Wilkins. Walters made his debut on 2 January 1988 in the Old Firm derby match with Celtic at Parkhead. His wasn't a day to remember as Rangers lost 2-0, and he was subjected to racist abuse from opposing Celtic fans who threw fruit onto the pitch. It was not unknown for him to retaliate to provocation, and he was ordered off twice in his early Rangers years, both times against Hearts at Tynecastle.

In the 1988-89 season when Rangers won the League title and the League Cup, the winger scored four times against Celtic, including in each of the 5-1 and 4-1 victories at Ibrox, and it was his wonderful shimmy and deep cross which set Mark Hateley up for his rampaging header in the title showdown with Aberdeen on the last day of the 1990-91 season. Enjoying the most successful spell of his career in terms of trophies won, Walters was not only a healthy provider for the Mo Johnston/Mark Hateley partnership in particular, but he scored more than his fair share of goals before being sold to Liverpool for £1.25 million—bringing Rangers a profit of £675,000.

His move to Anfield was somewhat ironic, seeing as his middle name is Everton! Souness had brought Walters back to England hoping he would terrorise defences as he had done in Scotland. But it wasn't to be, and he was an unused substitute in the 1992 FA Cup Final defeat of Sunderland and the 1995 League Cup Final win over Bolton Wanderers. Having had loan spells with Stoke and Wolves, he left Liverpool in January 1996 to join Southampton.

Having helped the Saints avoid relegation from the Premiership he joined Swindon Town, where his form at times could be mesmerising, but in other games he would go missing, a trait he hadn't been able to remove from his game since returning from Scotland. He later ended his career with Bristol Rovers, and is now head coach at Aston Villa's academy.

Although now officially retired, he still plays in the Sky Sports Masters football competitions for Rangers, where his dazzling displays are one of the highlights of the tournament. He is also an honorary member of the Rangers Supporters Trust.

## RAY WILKINS

**Born:** Hillingdon, 14 September 1956
**Rangers career:** 1987 to 1989
**Appearances and goals:**

| League | | FA Cup | | Lg Cup | | Europe | |
|---|---|---|---|---|---|---|---|
| A | G | A | G | A | G | A | G |
| 69/1 | 2 | 8 | 1 | 10 | 1 | 7 | 0 |

*Total appearances:* 94/1
*Total goals:* 4
**League Championships:** 1988-89; 1989-90
**League Cup:** 1988-89
**Honours:** 84 England caps

---

A complete thoroughbred, Ray Wilkins won the hearts and minds of the Ibrox faithful after arriving at Rangers from Paris St Germain in the autumn of 1987. He went on to prove himself an integral part of the Souness Revolution that paved the way for the nine-in-a-row success.

Captain of the England youth team, 'Butch' Wilkins joined Chelsea straight from school, and at the age of 18 became the Stamford Bridge club's youngest-ever captain. He led them to promotion to the First Division in 1976-77, but was unable to prevent their slide back to Division Two in 1978-79. By then a regular for England, going on to win 84 caps, Wilkins moved to Manchester United in the summer of 1979 for a fee of £825,000.

He spent five good years at Old Trafford, but he only had an FA Cup winners' medal to show for it, although he came close to winning the League Championship in his first season with the Reds.

In 1984 he joined the exodus to Italy, signing for AC Milan for £1.5 million. After three years he lost his place and moved to French club Paris St Germain. However, he hardly got a game in the French team and was rescued by Graeme Souness, who signed him for Rangers in November 1987. Wilkins repaid the Rangers boss with performances of consummate class and professionalism.

The midfielder missed very few games in his first two seasons at the club. As intelligent off the park as he was on it, Wilkins was the icing on the cake as in 1988-89 Rangers won the first of what was to become their record-equalling row of Championships. Wilkins won a place in the hearts of the Rangers faithful which probably owes as much to one moment of class as to his consistent performances. Rangers were being held 1-1 by reigning champions Celtic on a hot afternoon in August 1988. Wilkins smacked a tremendous right-foot volley into the top corner to give the Light Blues the momentum, which led eventually to them cruising to a 5-1 victory.

Perhaps that in itself accounts for the thunderous farewell ovation which he received from the 40,000 crowd on finally leaving the club after a home match against Dunfermline Athletic in November 1989.

Returning to London to play for Queen's Park Rangers, he made 182 appearances for the Loftus Road club before signing for Crystal Palace. But after just one game, he was back at Loftus Road as the club's player-manager. He later had a brief spell with Wycombe Wanderers before returning north of the border to play for Hibernian. He was brought back to the English game on a weekly contract, having brief spells with Millwall and Leyton Orient before finally hanging up his boots. After managing Fulham, he coached Chelsea and Watford before joining Millwall as assistant-manager. He now woorks as a pundit with Sky Sports.

## ALEC WILLOUGHBY

**Born:** Glasgow,
**Rangers career:** 1962 to 1969
**Appearances and goals:**

| League | | FA Cup | | Lg Cup | | Europe | |
|---|---|---|---|---|---|---|---|
| A | G | A | G | A | G | A | G |
| 70/5 | 39 | 4 | 1 | 11 | 6 | 5/1 | - |

*Total appearances:* 90/5
*Total goals:* 47
**League Cup:** 1963-64

Blond-haired inside-forward Alec Willoughby joined Rangers at the same time as his cousin Jim Forrest. The two of them had served a preliminary apprenticeship with Drumchapel Amateurs.

Though his first team opportunities during his early years at Ibrox were somewhat limited, he did replace the injured Jimmy Millar for the 1963-64 League Cup Final against Morton. While his cousin scored four of the goals in the 5-0 rout, Willoughby managed to grab Rangers' other goal. Two seasons later, having scored five goals to help the Light Blues reach yet another League Cup Final, he was on the losing side as Rangers went down 2-1 to Celtic.

Ironically, his real chance came after Rangers' infamous defeat at Berwick in January 1967, for which his cousin Jim Forrest was made the scapegoat. Willoughby was then converted from a stylish midfield player into a striker and most successful goalscorer.

In the games that followed the Berwick debacle, Willoughby netted consecutive League hat-tricks as both Hearts and Clyde were beaten 5-1. Less than a month later, Willoughby scored four of Rangers' goals in the 5-1 defeat of Motherwell. He ended that 1966-67 season with 16 goals in just 11 League starts as Rangers finished three points adrift of Champions Celtic. If he hadn't been dropped for decisive encounters late in the season, the Championship title might well have ended up at Ibrox.

A keen student of the game, Willoughby was hugely popular with the Rangers faithful, but he was inexplicably dropped in favour of Roger Hynd for the 1966-67 European Cup Winners' Cup semi-final second leg against Slavia Sofia and for the final itself against Bayern Munich in Nuremburg. Not surprisingly, the aggrieved forward immediately requested a transfer.

In hindsight, the treatment of Alec Willoughby towards the end of that season can be viewed as an error of judgement on the part of manager Scot Symon.

However, with the advent of new manager David White, Willoughby became more of a first team regular for the next couple of seasons, until the arrival of Andy Penman began to limit his chances. In May 1969, Willoughby was transferred to Aberdeen for a fee of £25,000, later leaving Pittodrie to play in Hong Kong.

When his playing career was over, Willoughby became manager of Rangers Supporters Social Club, just a stone's throw from the Ibrox ground. He later, along with Eric Caldow, hosted the new executive facilities at Ibrox.

# DAVIE WILSON

**Born:** Glasgow, 10 January 1939
**Rangers career:** 1956 to 1967
**Appearances and goals:**

| League | | FA Cup | | Lg Cup | | Europe | |
|---|---|---|---|---|---|---|---|
| **A** | **G** | **A** | **G** | **A** | **G** | **A** | **G** |
| 225/2 | 98 | 37/1 | 21 | 69/2 | 28 | 37 | 10 |

*Total appearances: 368/5*
*Total goals: 157*
**League Championships:** 1960-61; 1962-63
**Scottish Cup:** 1959-60; 1961-62; 1962-63; 1963-64; 1965-66
**League Cup:** 1960-61; 1961-62
**Honours:** 22 Scotland caps

Arguably Rangers' finest outside-left since the days of Alan Morton, Davie Wilson also had a natural striker's touch which made him dangerous in front of goal.

He joined Rangers from Baillieston Juniors in May 1956. A direct sort of player, one of Wilson's trademarks was to drift unseen into the box towards the far post when right-wingers Alex Scott or Willie Henderson were raiding down the right wing, and more often than not he would successfully convert their crosses. After making his League debut in January 1957 in a 3-1 defeat of Dundee, he had to bide his time for a couple of seasons before establishing himself in the second half of the League Championship-winning season of 1958-59.

Having appeared in only 15 games, he didn't qualify for a medal, but the following season he picked up his first silverware as Rangers beat Kilmarnock 2-0 in the Scottish Cup Final. He was particularly successful in the club's run to that final, netting a hat-trick against Berwick Rangers and two in the 4-1 semi-final replay victory over Celtic.

In 1960-61, Wilson played in every one of Rangers' 60 matches, picking up a League Championship medal and a League Cup Winners' medal after Kilmarnock had once again been beaten 2-0. He was also a member of the Rangers side that lost over two legs to Fiorentina in that season's European Cup Winners' Cup Final.

*Davie Wilson (www.snspix.com)*

Wilson was now reaching his peak, and midway through the 1961-62 season in which Rangers won both domestic cup competitions, he played centre-forward in the match at Falkirk as Jimmy Millar had dropped back to half-back. Wilson scored six goals against the Bairns as the Light Blues won 7-1, including three in the space of just eight minutes! Four days after this performance, he netted a hat-trick for the Scottish League in their 4-3 defeat of the Football League at Villa Park.

Wilson, who won 22 caps for Scotland, enjoyed two particularly satisfying games against England. The first was in 1962 when he scored Scotland's opening goal in a 2-0 win at Hampden, and the other a year later when 10-men Scotland won 2-1 at Wembley. That day his Rangers team-mate Eric Caldow had broken his leg and Wilson played with great distinction after moving to left-back.

The 1962-63 season was Davie Wilson's best in terms of goals scored, with 33 in all competitions including 23 in 32 League games as Rangers regained the Championship. That total included all four goals in a 4-1 win at Partick Thistle. He netted a hat-trick in the 6-0 Scottish Cup win over Airdrie, and then got one of the goals in the final as Rangers beat Celtic 3-0.

But as Rangers headed towards their first trophy in the Treble-winning season of 1963-64, tragedy struck when Wilson broke his ankle in the League Cup semi-final win over Berwick Rangers and had to sit out the final against Morton which Rangers won 5-0. The injury kept him out for five months, but he returned to help the Gers win the League title and received his fourth Scottish Cup winners' medal after Rangers triumphed over Dundee 3-1. He was to play in the Scottish Cup Final again in 1966 as Celtic were beaten 1-0 in a replayed final.

The 1966-67 season was to be Davie Wilson's last with the club, and though he scored the away goal against Slavia Sofia to put Rangers through to the European Cup Winners' Final, he did not play in the final itself, which Rangers lost 1-0 to Bayern Munich.

In the summer of 1967 he was transferred to Dundee United along with Wilson Wood, with Swedish international winger Orjan Persson coming in the opposite direction. He had a good number of seasons with the Tannadice club prior to becoming manager of Dumbarton. After three years in charge he moved to Kilmarnock as assistant manager, but returned to Dumbarton for a second spell before leaving to concentrate on his work in the whisky industry.

## WILLIE WOODBURN

**Born:** Edinburgh, 8 August 1919
**Died:** 2 December 2001
**Rangers career:** 1946 to 1955

**Appearances and goals:**

| | League | | FA Cup | | Lg Cup | | Europe | |
|---|---|---|---|---|---|---|---|---|
| | **A** | **G** | **A** | **G** | **A** | **G** | **A** | **G** |
| | 216 | 1 | 38 | 0 | 71 | 0 | - | - |

*Total appearances:* 325
*Total goals:* 1
**League Championships:** 1946-47; 1948-49; 1949-50; 1952-53
**Scottish Cup:** 1947-48; 1948-49; 1949-50; 1952-53
**League Cup:** 1946-47; 1948-49
**Honours:** 24 Scotland caps

One of the most gifted centre-halves that Rangers have ever had, it is unfortunate that Woodburn will always be remembered as the last professional player in Britain to have been banned indefinitely for indiscipline on the field.

Willie Woodburn played junior football for Edinburgh Ashton and signed professional for Rangers in October 1937. He made his League debut at the age of 20 in August 1938 as Rangers drew 2-2 with Motherwell. Rangers went on to lift the title, but Woodburn didn't qualify for a medal, having only played in 12 games.

After the war he established himself and in 1946-47 won the first of his four League Championship medals. That season also saw him appear in his first League Cup Final as Rangers beat Aberdeen 4-0. His form for the Light Blues led to him winning the first of 24 caps for Scotland when he played in the 1-1 draw against England at Wembley. Though the Scots led 1-0 at the interval, the second-half belonged to the home side, and it was only Woodburn's shackling of Tommy Lawton plus his goal-line clearance from Raich Carter that saved the day.

Over the next few seasons, Woodburn missed very few matches at international level and always seemed to save his best displays for the Auld Enemy. Two years later, at Wembley, he was a member of the Scotland team that had Morton keeper Jimmy Cowan to thank for a 3-1 win.

As a centre-half, Willie Woodburn was some thirty years ahead of his time. It is true that he was a hard and quite formidable tackler, strong in the air and full-blooded on the ground, but he could create as well as destroy. Woodburn's distribution from the back was extremely accurate, and he liked nothing better than to get forward and support his attack. Having said this, he scored just one goal in 325 appearances for the club, this coming in a 3-2 win at Motherwell towards the end of the 1950-51 season.

He was an extremely passionate player—he would verbally abuse his goalkeeper Bobby Brown for every goal he conceded, no matter how unstoppable the shot might have been!

Though his Rangers career was stormy, punctuated by a number of much-publicised brushes with authority, he was not a dirty player. He certainly had a temper, though, and in 1954 he was banned *sine die* for butting a Stirling Albion player. Most football historians believe that Willie Woodburn was made a scapegoat, a man punished in order to deter others—a fact possibly recognised by the Scottish FA when they lifted the ban almost three seasons later.

But by then it was too late for Woodburn—a superbly talented footballer—to resume playing. His career was over.

## CHRIS WOODS

**Born:** Boston, 14 November 1959
**Rangers career:** 1986 to 1991
**Appearances and goals:**

| League | | FA Cup | | Lg Cup | | Europe | |
|---|---|---|---|---|---|---|---|
| A | G | A | G | A | G | A | G |
| 173 | 0 | 15 | 0 | 21 | 0 | 21 | 0 |

*Total appearances:* 230
*Total goals:* 0
**League Championships:** 1986-87; 1988-89; 1989-90; 1990-91'
**League Cup:** 1986-87; 1988-89; 1990-91
**Honours:** 43 England caps

Goalkeeper Chris Woods was one of the earliest of a number of expensive purchases by Rangers boss Graeme Souness in what became known as the 'Souness era'.

Nottingham Forest beat a number of other clubs for the signature of this promising young keeper, and he sprang to fame in 1977-78 when Forest, newly promoted to Division One, ran away with the League Championship. However, he played no part in that particular triumph but starred in the club's first-ever League Cup victory. With Shilton cup-tied, Woods played in every match from the third round to the final, where he helped Forest win 1-0 in a replay after a goalless draw at Wembley. The following season he was selected for the England Under-21 side—the first player to be so honoured without a Football League appearance to his name.

Too good a keeper to remain Peter Shilton's understudy, he joined Queen's Park Rangers where he was first-choice until inexplicably losing his place to John Burridge. He moved on to Norwich City, and in 1984-85 won a second League Cup winners' medal. Although they were relegated that season, the Canaries bounced back as Second Division Champions, but Woods, who had just won his first full cap for England, did not stay for the next stint of top flight football and joined Rangers.

In the Championship season of 1986-87, his first with Rangers, he made many dramatic and outstanding saves and set a British record of successive games without conceding a goal—this run was brought to an end by the surprise home defeat by Hamilton Academical in a first round Scottish Cup tie at Ibrox in January 1987.

The following season, Woods was struck down by an uncommon and very persistent virus which seriously affected both his vision and balance, so much so that he missed almost half of that campaign. Then in the opening game of the following season against St Mirren, he damaged his right shoulder, which cost him more appearances.

Even so, in five seasons at Ibrox, Woods won four League Championship medals and three League Cup winners' medals. However, in 1991, Rangers reduced their contingent of English players to avoid problems with the UEFA ruling on 'foreigners' in European competition, and he was sold to newly promoted Sheffield Wednesday for £1.2 million.

In his first season at Hillsborough, the Owls finished third and almost stole the League title at the death. In 1992-93 he helped the Yorkshire club to both the FA Cup and League Cup Finals, but after that began to have a bad time with injuries. A brief loan spell at Reading followed before Woods left for a stint in the United States.

On his return to these shores he joined Southampton, but after half a dozen games, he broke his leg at Blackburn Rovers. On recovering, he joined Sunderland before signing for Burnley. Playing in a side facing relegation, he proved that much of his old ability was still in place, before injuries forced his retirement. He is now the goalkeeping coach at Premiership Everton.

## GEORGE YOUNG

**Born:** Grangemouth, 27 October 1922
**Died:** 10 January 1997
**Rangers career:** 1946 to 1957
**Appearances and goals:**

| League | | FA Cup | | Lg Cup | | Europe | |
|---|---|---|---|---|---|---|---|
| **A** | **G** | **A** | **G** | **A** | **G** | **A** | **G** |
| 293 | 22 | 50 | 5 | 83 | 4 | 2 | 0 |

*Total appearances:* 428
*Total goals:* 31
**League Championships:** 1946-47; 1948-49; 1949-50; 1952-53; 1955-56; 1956-57
**Scottish Cup:** 1947-48; 1948-49; 1949-50; 1952-53
**League Cup:** 1946-47; 1948-49;
**Honours:** 53 Scotland caps

Nicknamed 'Corky' because of the lucky champagne cork he carried, George Young was not just an illustrious Rangers captain but one of the most outstanding leaders in Scottish football.

Never sent off and booked only once, Young's introduction to the Ibrox club was, to say the least, a little fortuitous. He had played for a while for a

*After their playing days, former Rangers and Scotland stars George Young (left)
and Bob McPhail autograph a match ball at Ibrox (www.snspix.com)*

local club at the same time as a friend, an aspiring boxer as it happened, was
training at Falkirk's ground. The friend found he so liked football that he
became a goalkeeper and eventually signed for the Light Blues' junior club,
Kirkintilloch Rob Roy. He told his new club about Young—they had a look,
liked what they saw, and in 1941 they passed him on to Rangers.

George Young was Rangers' dominant figure during the middle part
of the century. A giant of a man in physical stature, in his influence on

the club and his personality, those who didn't see him play can gain some understanding by merely looking at the pictures of him leading Rangers or Scotland out as captain.

He was part of the famous Iron Curtain defence in the 1940s and 1950s which happened to comprise defensive experts such as Woodburn Shaw and Bobby Brown. Young's mammoth punts out of defence became part of Rangers' fairly simple counter-attack theory, but the Iron Curtain conceded only 180 goals in 180 games over six seasons.

Captain of Scotland 48 times, he also led his country to consecutive victories against England at Wembley—3-1 in 1949 and 3-2 in 1951.

Under Bill Struth, Young was largely in control of team matters, selection, tactics, training and so on and therefore can claim some additional credit for the 12 Championship, Cup and League Cup victories Rangers collected during his 428 games. Of all his silverware, perhaps none would be quite so fulfilling for him as the victory against Clyde in the 1949 Scottish Cup Final—Rangers won 4-1 and Young scored twice from the penalty spot. He was always a versatile player and, in 1953, played in goal to earn a draw and a successful replay against Aberdeen. And his fitness was such that between the autumn of 1948 and the summer of 1953, he missed a mere five League games out of the 150 Rangers played!

Young, who was a giant of the game in every sense, bowed out as a player at the end of the 1956-57 season and later had a brief spell managing Third Lanark.

He later retired to take over a hotel, keeping in touch with the game via the odd newspaper piece. No doubt it was a welcome break for a man who had broken his nose three times, his fingers once and had his leg in plaster on six occasions!

# RANGERS 100 HEROES TOP TENS

## LEAGUE

| | APPEARANCES | | | GOALS | |
|---|---|---|---|---|---|
| 1 | John Greig | 494/4 | 1 | Ally McCoist | 243 |
| 2 | Sandy Jardine | 431/20 | 2 | Willie Thornton | 139 |
| 3 | Ally McCoist | 331/57 | 3 | Derek Johnstone | 132 |
| 4 | Derek Johnstone | 357/12 | 4 | Ralph Brand | 127 |
| 5 | Ian McColl | 360 | 5 | Billy Simpson | 113 |
| 6 | Peter McCloy | 351 | 6 | Davie Wilson | 98 |
| 7 | Colin Jackson | 339/2 | 7 | Jimmy Millar | 92 |
| 8 | Alex Macdonald | 320/17 | 8 | Willie Johnston | 91 |
| 9 | Davie Cooper | 321 | 9 | Mark Hateley | 88 |
| 10 | Richard Gough | 318 | 10 | John Greig | 87 |

# RANGERS 100 HEROES TOP TENS

## SCOTTISH CUP

### APPEARANCES

| | | |
|---|---|---|
| 1 | John Greig | 72 |
| 2 | Sandy Jardine | 60/4 |
| 3 | Ian McColl | 59 |
| 4 | Derek Johnstone | 55/2 |
| 5 | Peter McCloy | 55 |
| 6 | Colin Jackson | 53 |
| 7 | Tommy McLean | 51 |
| 8= | George Young | 50 |
| | Alex Macdonald | 46/4 |
| 10 | Davie Cooper | 49 |

### GOALS

| | | |
|---|---|---|
| 1= | Derek Johnstone | 30 |
| | Jimmy Millar | 30 |
| 3 | Ralph Brand | 29 |
| 4 | Ally McCoist | 25 |
| 5= | Willie Thornton | 21 |
| | Davie Wilson | 21 |
| 7 | Max Murray | 19 |
| 8= | Alex Macdonald | 15 |
| | Billy Simpson | 15 |
| 10 | Tommy McLean | 12 |

# RANGERS 100 HEROES TOP TENS

## LEAGUE CUP

| APPEARANCES | | | GOALS | | |
|---|---|---|---|---|---|
| 1 | John Greig | 121 | 1 | Jim Forrest | 50 |
| 2 | Sandy Jardine | 106/1 | 2 | Ally McCoist | 45 |
| 3 | Ian McColl | 100 | 3 | Derek Johnstone | 39 |
| 4 | Peter McCloy | 86 | 4 | Ralph Brand | 38 |
| 5 | Derek Johnstone | 82/3 | 5 | Billy Simpson | 35 |
| 6= | Ronnie McKinnon | 83 | 6 | Willie Thornton | 29 |
| | George Young | 83 | 7= | Jimmy Millar | 28 |
| 8 | Alex Macdonald | 75/4 | | Davie Wilson | 28 |
| 9 | Davie Cooper | 69/8 | 9 | Sandy Jardine | 25 |
| 10 | Colin Jackson | 74/1 | 10 | Alex Scott | 24 |

# RANGERS 100 HEROES TOP TENS

## EUROPE

| APPEARANCES | | | GOALS | | |
|---|---|---|---|---|---|
| 1 | John Greig | 64 | 1 | Ally McCoist | 21 |
| 2 | Barry Ferguson | 53/1 | 2= | Jorg Albertz | 12 |
| 3 | Sandy Jardine | 50/2 | | Ralph Brand | 12 |
| 4 | Willie Henderson | 49/2 | | Jimmy Millar | 12 |
| | Ally McCoist | 42/9 | | Alex Scott | 12 |
| 6 | Ronnie McKinnon | 45 | 6= | Willie Henderson | 10 |
| 7 | Peter McCloy | 43 | | Alex Macdonald | 10 |
| 8 | Craig Moore | 42 | | Colin Stein | 10 |
| 9= | Lorenzo Amoruso | 40 | | Davie Wilson | 10 |
| | Willie Johnston | 40 | 10 | Derek Johnstone | 9 |

# RANGERS 100 HEROES TOP TENS

## OVERALL

| APPEARANCES | | GOALS | |
|---|---|---|---|
| 1 John Greig | 771/4 | 1 Ally McCoist | 334 |
| 2 Sandy Jardine | 647/27 | 2 Derek Johnstone | 210 |
| 3 Derek Johnstone | 525/21 | 3 Ralph Brand | 206 |
| 4 Davie Cooper | 465/76 | 4 Willie Thornton | 189 |
| 5 Peter McCloy | 535 | 5 Billy Simpson | 165 |
| 6 Ally McCoist | 435/81 | 6 Jimmy Millar | 162 |
| 7 Ian McColl | 526 | 7 Davie Wilson | 157 |
| 8 Colin Jackson | 503/3 | 8 Jim Forrest | 145 |
| 9 Alex Macdonald | 478/26 | 9 Max Murray | 121 |
| 10 Ronnie McKinnon | 473 | 10 Mark Hateley | 115 |